ALL IN
GOOD TIME

ALL IN GOOD TIME

When to Save, Stock Up,
and Schedule Everything
for Your Home

TARA KUCZYKOWSKI WITH
MANDI EHMAN

BERKLEY BOOKS, NEW YORK

THE BERKLEY PUBLISHING GROUP
Published by the Penguin Group
Penguin Group (USA) Inc.
375 Hudson Street, New York, New York 10014, USA
Penguin Group (Canada), 90 Eglinton Avenue East, Suite 700, Toronto, Ontario M4P 2Y3, Canada
(a division of Pearson Penguin Canada Inc.)
Penguin Books Ltd., 80 Strand, London WC2R 0RL, England
Penguin Group Ireland, 25 St. Stephen's Green, Dublin 2, Ireland (a division of Penguin Books Ltd.)
Penguin Group (Australia), 250 Camberwell Road, Camberwell, Victoria 3124, Australia
(a division of Pearson Australia Group Pty. Ltd.)
Penguin Books India Pvt. Ltd., 11 Community Centre, Panchsheel Park, New Delhi—110 017, India
Penguin Group (NZ), 67 Apollo Drive, Rosedale, Auckland 0632, New Zealand
(a division of Pearson New Zealand Ltd.)
Penguin Books (South Africa) (Pty.) Ltd., 24 Sturdee Avenue, Rosebank, Johannesburg 2196,
South Africa

Penguin Books Ltd., Registered Offices: 80 Strand, London WC2R 0RL, England

While the authors have made every effort to provide accurate telephone numbers and Internet addresses
at the time of publication, neither the authors nor the publisher assumes any responsibility for errors, or
for changes that occur after publication. Further, the publisher does not have any control over and does
not assume any responsibility for author or third-party websites or their content.

ALL IN GOOD TIME

Copyright © 2012 by Tara Kuczykowski and Mandi Ehman
Cover design by Diana Kolsky
Cover photos by Shutterstock
Book design by Tiffany Estreicher

First Edition: January 2012

ISBN 978-0-425-24516-3

An application to register this book for cataloging has been submitted to the Library of Congress

PRINTED IN THE UNITED STATES OF AMERICA

10 9 8 7 6 5 4 3 2 1

9753

For our husbands and children . . .
The reason we do what we do

CONTENTS

INTRODUCTION

This book isn't about frugal living or financial management. And it's not about tackling your time management skills so you can be more productive. What it *is* is a collection of tips and shortcuts that are sure to save you time and money here and there, as you choose, so that you'll have more of both to spend on the things and people that really matter to you.

If you can effortlessly juggle three square meals and several loads of laundry a day, keep your home spotless, volunteer for your favorite cause, shuttle yourself to the gym or your kids to Gymboree by day and the activity of the moment by night, all while keeping your budget in the black . . . if you can do all this, then you probably don't need any of the information you'll find here.

If, however, you—like us—struggle to find enough time and dollars to do everything on your to-do list while still making time for your family (not to mention for yourself) and getting a full night's sleep, we've written this book for you. If your budget never seems to stretch far enough to cover the groceries, the dentist bills, the extracurricular activities, and still leave you with some money for family vacations or to save, this book is for you too.

We've found that many people spend so much time and money on tasks and things when they could have saved minutes and dollars if they had only known to plan slightly differently. Why should you waste a Monday morning at the doctor's office for a regular checkup when you could be in and out in an hour on a Wednesday? Why spend several dollars on another gallon of gas when you can sign up for a grocery-store loyalty card that will save you money next time you're at the pump? It may only seem like a half hour here or a dollar there, but it all adds up.

ABOUT US

We met over six years ago, when Mandi had just become the new mom of a tiny baby girl and Tara was the mom of three little ones under three years old. We both worked a few hours a week from home, and we became fast friends even though we lived thousands of miles away from each other at the time.

Fast-forward six years, and we now have nine children ages nine years old and younger between us, work at home full-time, and our husbands, who share a passion for remote-controlled airplanes, are both stay-at-home dads.

Although we always laugh about the similarities between

our families, there are some pretty significant differences too. For example, Tara's four oldest attend public school, while Mandi and her husband homeschool their daughters. Tara and her family live in a suburban neighborhood in Ohio, while Mandi and hers live in rural West Virginia. And while Mandi's passions are organizing and productivity, Tara's passions are saving money and cooking from scratch without spending hours in the kitchen.

At the end of the day, we're both just busy moms trying to juggle all of our responsibilities. We know what it's like to be full-time home managers, and we know what it's like to be working moms. We've dealt with layoffs and unemployment and with active sports schedules and busy workdays.

ABOUT THIS HANDBOOK

As we said at the beginning, this book is a resource for busy households looking for ways to trim their schedules and their budgets without giving up the things they love. We don't expect anyone to implement every single tip or idea we have, but we're including them all in here so that you can pick and choose what works for you and your family at any given time.

The "as *you* choose" part is an important part of both of our philosophies. It's easy to get caught up in the idea of saving every penny you can or having a perfectly organized home or being productive all the time. We believe those are all good things—within reason. But we also believe in splurging (when we can afford it) to take our families to Disney World and making time for impromptu backyard campfires or games of Candy Land with our kids. Wouldn't you rather spend an extra half hour outside with your kids than in a germy doctor's office? To us, that's the goal of saving time and money—not to prove that we can hang with the best, but to leave more for our families.

Whether you're a working mom, a stay-at-home parent, or something in between, there are probably times when you feel stretched—financially, emotionally, and physically. We want to show you how to stretch your resources and your minutes rather than yourself. We've all heard the adage that children are only young once, and it's true. Our babies are toddlers and elementary aged now, and we know it won't be long before they're preteens and high schoolers and then moving out on their own. We want to do what we can to maximize our time and money to make as many enduring and happy memories as we can while they're still ours!

HOW TO USE IT

This handbook is broken down by room as we tackle everything from the rec room (aka: family time, vacations, and entertainment) to the backyard (aka: lawn care, landscaping, and outdoor play). In each section, we'll tackle the most common purchases and tasks and share our tips for saving time and money, as well as some fun extras such as Tara's secret recipe for homemade Clorox Anywhere and Mandi's ten questions for decluttering. There's also a bonus section for holiday planning since the holidays notoriously take their toll on our schedules, stress levels, and budgets.

Flip through the book for ideas that every family can use, focus on one section at a time, or search for a specific area you've already identified as a pain point.

We hope that *All in Good Time* will be a trusted resource that you refer to over and over again. We've both made it our personal mission to share our tips and ideas with other home managers, and this book is a compilation of all of our very best tips.

CREDITS

We've been part of forums, email groups, and the blogosphere since before we had kids, and over the last ten years, we've learned so much from other families. It would be impossible to trace back all of the tips we've gleaned from other people to their original source since a lot of these ideas have been shared multiple times. Our goal in this book is to share these same ideas with others and keep the tradition going.

In the cases where we didn't have tips of our own to share, we've asked some of our favorite bloggers to share their tips. One thing we love about the blogosphere is that there's so much to learn from other people, and we appreciate that each of them was willing to share their expertise with you as well!

AFFILIATE LINKS

Throughout the book, we've included quick links to help you find the information, product, or service we're referring to. Some—but certainly not all—of these contain affiliate links, which means we earn a tiny percentage if you make a purchase through those links. However, links have been added based on their relevance and usefulness to you, not on whether an affiliate link was available, and we stand behind each and every recommendation!

Your Home

BUILDING A NEW HOME

Building a new home is exciting, but it's also a lot of work! Mandi's family built their home while she was pregnant with their third daughter, moving in just weeks before she gave birth. That's not something we recommend! As we're writing this, Tara's family is trying to decide between building and buying a new home, knowing there are benefits and drawbacks to each.

When building, you have more control over the details, big and small. If you build in a "cookie-cutter" neighborhood, your choices may be limited to colors and lighting, but if you build in an area with fewer restrictions, you can customize everything to your heart's content.

When Mandi and her husband built their residence, they decided to go with a manufactured home. Their home was literally built in four pieces in a factory and then pieced together on-site. Even through this process, they were able to customize the layout to fit their family's needs and add custom flooring and handmade barn-style sliding doors.

Building a home can save you money, but you can also be hit with a lot of unexpected expenses, so it's important to be realistic about your budget going in. Unless you're experienced in the construction industry, it's best to hire a general contractor who can help you navigate the waters of permits, quotes, and subcontractors.

Save money by doing some of the legwork yourself. For example, Mandi and her husband purchased their own kitchen cabinets and appliances and installed them themselves. On a smaller scale, even installing your own faucets and fixtures can save you money. However, like anything, you'll trade money for time and stress, and only you know which is more important to your family.

You can also save money by purchasing some of the materials you need on eBay (yes, eBay!), as factory overstock, or directly from manufacturers rather than through retailers. Habitat for Humanity's ReStore outlets can be found throughout the United States, and they sell tons of surplus materials— including building materials, furniture, accessories, and appliances—at a fraction of retail price. We're both huge fans of IKEA, and they sell cabinets, fixtures, and even flooring at reasonable prices.

BUYING A HOME

As clichéd as it sounds, the right time to buy a home is when you're ready—emotionally and financially. You may be looking to buy a home (or new home) as an investment, to accommodate your growing family, or to move out of a not-so-great neighborhood, which are all good reasons. However, as we've seen from the last couple of years, it's important not to stretch your budget too tightly in order to do it, because there are no guarantees and it could end up hurting you in the short and long term.

When buying a home, you'll typically find the most inventory in the spring and early summer, but there will also be more competition for the best homes on the market. In the fall and winter, you'll have less competition and may be able to negotiate more with sellers, but you'll have less to choose from. A real-estate agent can walk you through the particular trends in the area where you're looking to buy and help you negotiate and protect yourself throughout the process. The seller pays the agents involved in a transaction once a sale is made, so there's really not a downside to using an agent to help you find the right home.

CLEANING

There are a dozen theories on how and when to clean your home, from FlyLady to Martha Stewart to the Clutter Diet.

Although each of these systems is great and works well for tons of people, the real key is to find the right system for *you*. Think about the traffic patterns in your home, your daily and weekly schedule, and your own preferences. Do you prefer to clean a little bit each day or to set aside a couple of hours once a week to clean the house top to bottom? The easiest way to start creating your system is to make a list of the daily, weekly, monthly, and yearly chores that need to be done and then start creating routines to get them done.

Although it sounds overwhelming, Mandi's found that working together as a family to straighten the house each night before bed keeps things from building up. Everyone—from the toddler to her husband—has a job, and they get to spend time together while working through their chores. Each morning they wake up to a relatively straight home, even if it's not always perfectly clean, which eliminates a lot of stress.

While routines are important, we all know that sometimes things get behind schedule and out of control. A great strategy for quickly regaining control is the fifteen-minute blitz. When things start to get out of control and you start to feel over-whelmed, set your timer for fifteen minutes and blitz through your home, starting with those areas that have the biggest impact, cleaning up as much as possible within that time limit. The more often you blitz, the easier it will be to stay on top of clutter, and you can even wipe down the bathroom sink or dust the living area as part of your blitz once or twice a week.

Laundry baskets make great tools for carrying stuff from one room to the next as you straighten and clean. Focus your attention on one room—filling the basket with anything that belongs somewhere else—rather than running back and forth between rooms as you go. Tara's family also utilizes pretty baskets on the steps leading upstairs. They get filled throughout the day and everyone puts away their basket at night before bed.

CLEANING SUPPLIES

The best way to save money on your cleaning supplies is to make your own! Not only are homemade cleaners a fraction of the cost of commercial cleaners, but they're safer for your family and the environment as well. For kitchen and bathroom sinks and surfaces, a spray bottle with vinegar is all you really need, and a microfiber cloth is great for dusting. See the appendix for more specialized homemade cleaner recipes.

Of course, if you'd still rather purchase your cleaners, you still have options, but watch out for "green-washed" products that claim to be natural, organic, or safe but still contain long lists of sketchy ingredients. Tara really likes Method products, especially the pink grapefruit all-purpose spray and the Best In Glass Cleaner in mint. You'll find occasional Method coupons as well as frequent sales at Amazon.com and Soap.com.

CLOSET ORGANIZERS

Like other organizational products, closet organizers tend to be at their lowest prices in January when everyone seems to be resolving to get organized in the New Year.

Closet organizers, containers, and other organizational products are a huge industry for one simple reason: so many people purchase them thinking that having the right product will solve their organizational woes. Unfortunately, that's not true, and oftentimes the product that seemed perfect on the store shelves doesn't work quite as well in the actual space you're trying to organize. Rather than spending money on your organizers up front, start by decluttering and organizing your things so that you'll have a better idea of what will fit your needs.

MOVING

Mandi and her husband moved four times in the first five years they were married—including two cross-country moves—so they have a few tips to share in this area.

To save on packing costs, ask your local grocery store or big-box retailer to save merchandise boxes for you. These are broken down as they're unpacked each day, so your best bet is to call early in the morning and ask them to save boxes for you. Each store's policies on this will vary, so call the customer-service desk to see what they have available. For fragile or heavy items, stop by a local liquor store and ask for any old boxes they have since these boxes are typically smaller and much sturdier.

You don't always have a lot of control over when you move since expiring leases, real-estate settlements, and work schedules all play a role in scheduling a move. However, there are definitely better times to move. Because families with children are most likely to move during the summer months, you'll find more availability and lower prices during the school year. Similarly, because new leases and rentals often start at the beginning of the month, you'll also find more availability and lower costs in the middle of the month. Finally, you'll find better prices on moving trucks on Tuesday and Wednesday since most people tend to move on the weekends.

Of course, the best way to save on moving costs is simply to do it yourself with the help of family and friends. For a small to medium-size household, a few pickup trucks and a couple of trips back and forth will get the job done!

For moves between states or cross-country moves, Mandi highly recommends Movex.com, a self-service moving service that contracts with tractor-trailer drivers to carry your load when their trucks might otherwise be empty. It's a self-service move in that you're still responsible for loading and unloading your goods, but they take care of the actual driving so that you can drive your own vehicles or fly to your new home. Mandi and her husband used this service when they moved to Utah in 2003 and again when they moved back east in 2005, and they were extremely impressed with both the price and efficiency of the service. The price is based on the amount of space you'll need in the truck (and their handy calculator will help you make that estimation), and they actually have movable walls inside the truck that allow them to pick up and drop off multiple loads on the way, which is how they keep the cost so low.

Moving Checklist

EIGHT WEEKS BEFORE YOUR MOVE:
- Have school records transferred to the new school district.
- Get copies of medical, dental, legal, and financial records.
- Call your insurance agent to discuss the effects of your move on your policies.

SIX WEEKS BEFORE YOUR MOVE:
- Begin collecting boxes.
- Create a folder or binder to organize all of your receipts, inventories, etc.
- Make a list of people to notify about your move.

FOUR WEEKS BEFORE YOUR MOVE:
- Set an actual moving day and arrange for truck rental, help from friends and family, etc.
- Arrange to have your current utilities transferred or disconnected and to have the new ones connected.
- File a change of address with the post office.
- Begin packing, clearly labeling each box with its contents and which room it belongs in.

TWO WEEKS BEFORE YOUR MOVE:
- Take giveaway items to the local thrift shop.
- Confirm truck rentals or moving arrangements.
- Use up any perishables in your fridge or freezer.
- Create a low-stress meal plan for moving week.
- Have your cars serviced, especially if you're doing an interstate move or it's been a while since your last service.

THE WEEK BEFORE YOUR MOVE:
- Pack your suitcase and any "open this first" boxes of essentials.
- Make arrangements for child care on moving day.
- Clean appliances, defrost the freezer.

MOVING DAY:
- Start the day with a healthy breakfast so you have energy for the move.
- Get rid of any trash that might add to the clutter and chaos of moving day.
- Keep a list of cell-phone numbers for the people helping with your move, whether they're friends and family or professional movers, so that you can get in touch with them as needed.
- Designate someone to direct traffic and oversee the move, especially if you have multiple people helping.
- Once the house is empty, check to make sure the a/c or heat is turned off, the water is turned off, all lights are turned off. Check the refrigerator, cabinets, closets, attic, basement, and crawl spaces for any last-minute items.

AFTER YOUR MOVE:
- Register for new tags, get a new driver's license, and register to vote.
- Notify any creditors or subscription holders that you haven't yet notified to give them your new address.
- Contact your local newspaper to set up a new subscription.

ORGANIZING

Having an organized home saves you time and money because you can find what you need when you need it, and you don't have to spend extra time cleaning clutter or sorting through stuff.

However, getting organized isn't an overnight process. If you look at your home as a whole and write "get organized" on your to-do list, you're going to fail. There are too many drawers, cabinets, and crevices where stuff hides for you to tackle this project as a whole. Instead, start by choosing one room in your home. Now pick one drawer or cabinet in that room. That is where you should start. Completely clean out, declutter, and organize that space and then move on to the next.

If you truly want to get organized, there's no way around decluttering. You have to look at your stuff with a discerning eye and make the hard decisions about what to keep and what to get rid of. Even the most organized system loses its effectiveness when you are overwhelmed by stuff, and the less stuff you have, the easier it will be to get organized.

A common mistake when trying to organize a space is to simply move things around within the drawer or between drawers and cabinets. To create an organizational system that is easy to use and will last, try pulling everything out of the space you're organizing. Set it on a flat surface such as the floor or counter so that you can see all of it at once. Then begin grouping like items and thinking about where things should be put away so that you can easily find them. Starting with a blank slate gives you room to start fresh without the constraints of your old system. It also becomes a motivating factor of its own. Because you start with a clean, uncluttered area, you're more likely to think twice about every item you put back in it, which helps in the decluttering process.

Getting organized will last only if you find a system that works for you. Sure, you could replicate a Martha Stewart system perfectly, and it would look organized. But chances are that you won't be able to maintain it because it's not your system and it doesn't take your needs, preferences, and lifestyle into consideration. Don't let yourself become discouraged by the idea that you have to achieve this organizing nirvana in order to be truly organized. Instead, create your own systems that reflect your personality and vision for the space. Find tips and tricks for every area of your home in Laura Wittman's *Clutter Rehab* (http://allingoodtime.net/clutterrehab).

To save money while organizing, hold off on buying any containers until after you've organized and know exactly what you need. Our local dollar stores have tons of containers for just $1 each, although you may want to invest in nicer baskets or boxes when they will sit out in the open. Either way, wait to make your purchases so you don't end up with sizes or styles that don't help as much as the right ones would!

Decluttering

One aspect of having a simple home is to keep it free from clutter. While there are varying degrees of this and not everyone chooses to live a minimalist lifestyle, there's no way to get around the need to declutter regularly to prevent your home from being overrun with stuff. Here are ten questions to ask yourself as you evaluate each item in your home:

1. Is this item something I use regularly?
2. If not, is it something I love?
3. Am I keeping this out of obligation or expectation?
4. Am I holding on to this because I think I should love it?
5. Am I saving this just in case?
6. Do I have multiples of the same thing?
7. Could something else I own do the same job?
8. Am I holding on to a broken item to fix one day?
9. Is this item worth the time I spend cleaning/storing it?
10. Could I use this space for something else?

PAINT

Freshen up a room with a new paint color without spending a lot of money by choosing your colors from the paint returns at your local home improvement store. These sell for as low as $1 a gallon, a great deal if you're not picky about the exact color you're getting. It may be hard to match these colors at a later time, so keep that in mind for high traffic areas or large rooms, or consider picking them up for an accent wall rather than to paint the entire room.

REMODELING

Remodeling, like building a new home, is a time-intensive project that often includes hidden costs. To get the best deals on labor, always shop around for quotes and be willing to haggle for a lower price. Like building a new home, you'll save money by shopping around for your materials as well. Check eBay, factory overstock outlets, and compare the prices at your local hardware stores.

Andrea Dekker from SimpleOrganizedLiving.com recently remodeled her dream home, a 120-year-old farmhouse, and she shares these tips for remodeling without busting your budget or losing your mind:

- Before you open a can of paint or even purchase a paintbrush, create an "idea book" with color schemes, room layouts, fixtures, styles, and decor you like. Just the simple act of filling a book with pictures that catch your attention is a great way to help you define your style.

- If you're remodeling a new-to-you home, live with the space for a while before you begin working on it. Even if you can hardly stand it, don't renovate until you've really had a chance to live in, use, and learn about the space so that you can make the best choices about what you really need and want.

- It's important to remember that many of the beautifully decorated homes in magazines aren't practical for families, pets, real life, cold climates, or anyone who can't afford a half-dozen staff! Choose designs, fabrics, and materials that suit your family, your life, your climate, and your budget. Beautiful isn't bad, but it's important to be realistic too.

- Although it's important to seek advice from professionals and you'll benefit from hearing from friends, family, and acquaintances about what they like and dislike in their homes, always go with what you love, even if it's nontraditional or unpopular with the people around you. You're the one who will be living with it every day, not them!

- Finally, be sure to do the first things first. Even if your main focus is to install bead-board paneling on the walls, think a little further down the road. Will you need to install any new windows? If so, you'll want to do that *before* you put up the paneling. Do you want to replace the carpet with wood floors? If so, that should all be done *before* the paneling. Think through everything you want to do before you start. Not only will you work more efficiently, but you'll save money as well.

SPRING CLEANING

Spring cleaning is a great time to refresh your home, figuratively and literally, after keeping it shut up during the winter. Open the windows and create a plan to work through each area or room in your home one by one. If you have small children and other daily obligations, deep cleaning the whole house in one day is probably not realistic. Instead, focus on one room at a time over several weeks, taking time to declutter and clean as you go. In *Organized Simplicity* (http://allingoodtime.net/organizedsimplicity), Tsh Oxenreider provides tips and strategies for spring cleaning every room in your house. It's a great read!

Sample Cleaning Schedule

DAILY:
- dishes
- laundry
- put away toys
- sweep/vacuum kitchen floor
- wipe counters
- wipe bathroom sinks after use
- sort mail

WEEKLY:
- wipe down kitchen appliances and other surfaces
- empty and wipe down trash cans
- clean out the fridge and freezer
- vacuum or sweep
- change bed linens
- dust
- clean glass
- clean toilets, tubs, and sinks

MONTHLY:
- deep-clean microwave, oven, and refrigerator
- wash rugs

- disinfect handles, door knobs, railings and light switch covers
- dust air vents, light fixtures, and ceiling fans
- change or clean furnace and vacuum filters

SEASONALLY:
- clean window treatments
- clean windows

Backyard

BICYCLES

New models come out in early spring, so the best time to purchase bicycles is after the holiday season when stores are anxious to get rid of their overstock to make room for the new inventory. However, bicycles are readily found at garage sales and thrift stores, so purchasing a gently used bike may be a better option, especially for casual riders or small children who will quickly outgrow them.

TIP: While it may be tempting to purchase larger bikes that children will grow into, it's better to purchase a less expensive bike that fits them at their current stage so that they can really develop the motor skills necessary to ride a bike rather than struggle with a bike that's too big. To save money, purchase gender-neutral models that can be passed down through each of your children as they grow!

Storage

Bikes take up a lot of room—especially if you have several children—so Tara's husband hung their family's bikes from the ceiling of the garage with Rubbermaid bike hooks. The bikes are high enough that cars can still pull into the garage but low enough that Tara or her husband can easily reach up and lift them down.

If you'd rather keep your bikes down lower, try a standing bike rack that allows you to line up bikes to prevent them from getting tangled or knocked over.

Helmets

Helmets are an important safety measure, and all children should wear one when riding their bike. It's important that helmets fit properly, snuggly touching the head all the way around with the helmet level and held snugly by the strap.

May is Bicycle Safety Month, and you may see sales and specials on helmets during that month. If you purchase a bike from a smaller bike shop, try negotiating for a discount on your helmet as well. Helmets may be passed down from child to child, but you'll want to be sure they've never been in a crash and that they meet current Consumer Product Safety Commission (CPSC) standards.

BOATS

Whether you're heading out for fishing, waterskiing, or just to relax on the water, boating is a great activity for the whole family. Mandi's family spent a significant amount of time boating when she was a kid, towing their boats—*Double Delight* and *bayQuest DSV*—back and forth from their home to the Chesapeake Bay. If you ask Mandi's dad about boating as a family, you're likely to hear the story of the time young Mandi almost drove the boat into a lighthouse. But we dug a little deeper to get some of his tips for buying, owning, safely operating, and storing a boat.

The first thing you should know is that boat prices are lowest during the off-season—when long days and warm temps are a distant memory. You'll find the best prices from manufacturers and private sellers in January, February, and March during the winter boat-show season. This is true even in warmer areas of the country as manufacturers try to clear out their inventory to make room for new models. Like cars, though, boats depreciate very quickly, so your best bet for getting a deal is to buy used.

Before You Buy

Consider how you'll use the boat before deciding on a size or model. Will you be fishing, cruising, or waterskiing? How many people do you want to be able to accommodate? Do you want a cabin for preparing food, sleeping, and overnight trips? Your answer to each of these questions affects the type, size, and cost of the boat you'll need.

There are several costs involved with owning a boat; you will need to dock it, store it in a boatel, or tow it to and from the marina, each of which has pros and cons and different price points. Boats require more maintenance than cars, so you'll need to budget for that as well as the purchase price and storage costs.

TIP: Some states require you to take a safe boating course before operating a boat, but even if yours doesn't, you may want to consider taking one. You'll learn about safe practices, the costs of operating a boat, and other considerations to keep in mind. Before heading out on the water, always make sure you have U.S. Coast Guard–approved life jackets for everyone. As a bonus, taking a safety class may qualify you for a discount on your boat insurance premium, as will having a clean driving record!

CARS

When it comes to cars, we've both had our fair share over the years. If your heart is set on a new car, the best time to buy is in the early fall, when new models hit the floor and dealers are anxious to get rid of the older models.

Your best bang for your buck, however, is to buy used. According to financial guru Dave Ramsey, cars depreciate an average of 60 to 70 percent over the first four years, and you can pick up company-leased cars, repos, and other used cars in great condition and with low miles for much less than a new car.

Extended Warranty

These days, both new and used car purchases from dealerships include offers for extended warranties. Like electronic warranties, though, a *Consumer Reports* survey has shown that they're not usually worth the cost. Consider what happened to Tara and her family . . . They bought a used car warranty that sounded like a good deal but was really worthless. They bought a car in mid-February and used the sunroof for the first time at the beginning of April. The sunroof worked a few times and then broke. At first they were told the damages were covered, and then they were told that since the problem wasn't specifically with the sunroof motor, it was not. The dealership wanted more than $1,000 to fix a little plastic piece on the track that had snapped, and would not budge, so they never had it fixed.

TIP: Instead of purchasing the extended warranty, set aside that same amount of money in savings for unexpected repairs. If you were planning to finance the warranty with the cost of the car, make an extra monthly payment into a sinking fund for car repairs.

Gas

With gas prices on the rise, gas is a significant part of many household budgets, but there are ways to save on this expense. The most obvious is to simply stay home. Except that's not exactly possible when you're running a household. So run errands once a week rather than spreading them out over several days, and plan your weekly menu and grocery list so that you're not making last-minute runs to the grocery store. You'll deal with fewer people on the road and in the stores during the week as opposed to weekends, so pick a weekday for errands if you can!

You can also save gas while driving. When possible, avoid stop-and-go traffic by taking alternate routes and avoiding rush hour. When you do start driving, accelerate slowly rather than peeling off the line. Empty your car of unnecessary clutter to save gas as well since the heavier your car, the more gas you use. Keeping your tires properly inflated and using your cruise control will also improve your gas mileage and save you money.

Obviously, carpooling is a great way to save on gas expense and wear and tear on your car. Even if you don't work outside the home, or carpooling to work isn't an option, look for car pools for your kids for school, sports activities, or other events.

TIP: Save on the gas that you do buy with your grocery-store loyalty cards. Many stores offer customers the opportunity to earn per-gallon discounts based on their purchases during the promotion period. If you do all of your shopping at one store, you can save 20 cents to a dollar per gallon on a single fill-up every few months through these promotions. Gift-card purchases usually count toward these promotions, so purchase cards for other businesses that you regularly visit—restaurants, retail stores, etc.—as a way to increase your gas savings.

If you purchase a lot of gas or are brand loyal, consider a gas credit card, which rewards you over time with special discounts on all of your purchases. If you're not brand loyal, visit GasBuddy.com to find information on the least expensive gas stations in your area.

Insurance

To get the lowest car insurance premiums possible, start by comparing prices online. Your driving record, credit report, and even report card (for teens and college students) play a role in your car insurance rates, so be sure to get updated quotes regularly from various companies to be sure your current policy is still the best deal. When possible, purchase both your car and homeowner's insurance from the same provider for additional discounts. You'll also pay less when you pay your six-month premiums in full rather than splitting them into monthly payments. Finally, also consider raising your deductible, which can significantly reduce your coverage cost, but it's important to make sure you can actually afford the higher deductible.

TIP: Whenever you purchase a new vehicle, be sure to call your insurance agent and get a quote on coverage before you buy. Some makes and models cost significantly more to insure than others, and you don't want to get stuck with an insurance payment that you can't really afford. If you drive an older vehicle that is paid in full, it probably doesn't make sense to keep comprehensive coverage. Instead, put the difference in premiums directly into a sinking fund for car repairs and replacement.

Maintenance

The very best way to save on maintenance is to roll up your sleeves and do as much of the preventive maintenance as you can yourself. This includes oil changes, keeping your tires properly inflated, and adding windshield-washer fluid. If you're not a do-it-yourselfer, sign up for the mailing lists of your local dealers and quick service shops because you'll receive coupons and sales flyers that can save you money. One final way we save is by using coupon booklets like the Entertainment Book (http://allingoodtime.net/entertainmentbook) or those sold through local fund-raisers, and a lot of times you'll even find free oil changes and maintenance offers in these.

Although most of us think of oil changes as an "every 3,000 miles" thing, *Shop Smart* magazine says that most newer cars can actually go up to 7,500 miles between oil changes without any problem. Check your owner's manual for details on the appropriate schedule for your make and model.

When shopping for the best price on tires, it helps to know specifically which tires you're interested in purchasing so that you can then call around to various shops to get their best offer. Watch for the "buy three get one free" deals that many shops have or for package deals that include lifetime warranties and free rotate and balance with purchase. Mandi's family usually purchases their tires from TireRack.com and then has a local shop put them on.

TIP: If you only need to purchase a single tire to replace a flat, consider calling around to junkyards or shops that offer gently used tires. Chances are you can find a match with a little wear on it that will last until you need to purchase four new tires, and you'll pay just a fraction of retail.

When taking your car into a shop for maintenance, it's important to find a mechanic whom you trust to be honest and do quality work. Mandi's stepdad, who used to own a chain of tire shops, says that the best way to find a trustworthy shop is to start with your local AAA, Department of Consumer Affairs, or Better Business Bureau. For more expensive repairs, don't be afraid to get a second opinion before agreeing to have any work done. Over time, you'll develop a relationship with a shop and may not feel the need to continue getting second opinions, but in the beginning, it's better safe than sorry.

Selling a Car

Gone are the days when you could just slap a "For Sale" sign in the window of your car or place an ad in your local paper. The best way to sell a car today is online. Start by cleaning up the car inside and out and taking care of any minor repairs that you can make yourself. Estimate the value via Kelley Blue Book, and list your car easily on sites like eBay Motors, Cars Direct.com, or AutoTrader.com.

Tara and her husband sold their thirtieth-anniversary Camaro Z28 on eBay when they found out they were expecting their third child. The process was fairly simple and easy, though not necessarily painless since they loved that car, and Tara admits to shedding a few tears when the buyer drove off in it!

Wherever you list your car, be sure to describe it in great detail. Not only will this cut down on the number of emails you receive, but it will also give potential buyers confidence, especially those who may be bidding sight unseen on eBay. Make sure to disclose any issues with the car up front, and take lots of pictures. Photograph the car from multiple angles inside and out, including close-ups of any problem areas. If you don't have a high-quality camera, it's a good idea to borrow one because clear and crisp pictures will result in more attention and, ultimately, more bids.

Winter Car-Care Tips

- Wipe headlights with car wax to prevent road spray from building up on your headlights.
- Soak a cloth in rubbing alcohol or ammonia and wipe your windshield wipers to fix streaking and squeaking.
- Spray windows with a mixture of three parts vinegar to one part water each night to prevent layers of ice from accumulating overnight.

- Spray cooking oil on the rubber seals around car doors and rub it in with a paper towel to prevent water from soaking in and freezing your doors shut.
- Spray shaving cream or vinegar on the inside of your windshield and wipe clean to prevent fogging.
- To instantly deice car locks, put hand sanitizer gel on your key and the lock.
- Increase your car's traction by putting a bag or two of cat litter in the trunk. If you do get stuck, you'll be able to use the litter to get out.

Car Rentals

To save money when renting a car, get an estimate up front. Be sure to ask about special offers and discounts and call around to several companies so you can compare pricing. Find out whether there are any additional fees or extra charges that may not be obvious. In most cases you can opt out of the insurance if you already have auto insurance, as the rental should be covered under your current policy, but you'll want to verify this with your agent. Since there's no cancellation penalty with most companies as long as you cancel ahead of time, the best strategy for saving is to book right away and then check periodically for better rates.

DECKS & PATIOS

Adding a deck or patio not only improves the livability of your home but actually adds to its value and salability too. The best time to add a patio or deck is off-season, typically November through February, although this can vary depending on where you live. Although you won't see as much seasonal fluctuations in materials as you might see on other purchases, contractors have more availability in the off-season and are more likely to negotiate on their prices.

TIP: To save even more money, consider building your own patio or deck. Tara's husband and a neighbor built their three-hundred-square-foot deck for just $1,200 and a few days' worth of work!

Maintenance

Wash or pressure-wash your deck each spring so that you can enjoy it all year long. While you're at it, inspect the rails and slats for any loose or broken pieces that should be replaced. Depending on the weather where you live, you'll want to apply a fresh finish coat to your deck every one to four years to keep it fresh and protected.

GARAGE SALES/ YARD SALES/TAG SALES

When you're clearing out a lot of clutter, a garage sale is an easy way to sell more all at once. However, for higher-priced items, such as furniture and collectibles, you may do better selling on Craigslist, Amazon, or eBay.

The best time to have a garage sale is from April through June, before the weather gets too hot, or in September, as the weather starts to cool. In many cities, garage sales now start on Thursday or Friday and run through the weekend as a way to appeal to more buyers and sell more. Garage sales held after the first and fifteenth of the month often do slightly better since many people get paid on those days.

The key to a successful yard sale is planning and preparation. The more you prepare, the more money you'll walk away with. You may want to invest in a paid ad in the newspaper or on a classified site dedicated solely to garage sales (http://allin goodtime.net/garagesales). Additionally, put flyers up at grocery stores, schools, and community centers ahead of time to draw buyers. On the day of your sale, proper signage is important. Use large signs with large, clear writing and arrows for people to follow to your sale. For the best results, avoid colorful signs (big black letters on white poster board is best), signs with too many words, or signs drawn by children.

To prepare for your sale, pack things up by category as you're decluttering your home so that you know what is in each box or bag and items are already grouped when it's time to unpack them. Price items reasonably so that you don't have a ton of leftovers at the end of the day. You'll still want to leave room for negotiating, but clothing priced at $5 per piece is probably not the best way to actually make a ton of sales. Once you decide on pricing, clearly mark items with price stickers so that browsers don't have to ask you the price of every item you're selling.

Make sure you have plenty of plastic grocery bags for buyers when they "check out" as well as sufficient cash on hand to make change. We recommend that you avoid pricing items below 25 cents so that you don't have to deal with pennies, nickels, and dimes.

TIP: Planning for the stuff that's left at the end of the day is almost as important as planning for the actual sale. Rather than taking it back into the house, we immediately load everything into our cars and drop it off at a local thrift shop, but you may want to keep any high-value items and try to sell them through other avenues before doing that.

GARDEN

There's no doubt that growing your own produce can save money and give you peace of mind if you're looking for organic, nongenetically modified food. Gardening does involve an investment of time and money, though, so it may not be for everyone.

You'll find the best deals on garden tools in March before the growing season starts. As with most things, you'll get a better price when you buy dirt by the truckload, so arrange to go in with your neighbors and split the cost.

Planning

Shaina from FoodforMyFamily.com recommends that you start preparing your garden in the fall so that you're ready to go when the ground thaws the following spring. Plants should be moved outside after the frost date for your area, which you can find through the National Climatic Data Center (http://allingoodtime.net/NCDC). If you're starting from seeds, start with your area's frost date and calculate backward based on the recommended planting time for each variety.

There are several different ways to simplify the gardening process, depending on the size of the garden you want to grow. Tara's family has a Backyard Botanical Oasis Garden (http://allingoodtime.net/oasis), which allows them to grow their own produce with minimal effort as far as weeding, watering, etc. They have the largest size to give them space to grow plenty of fresh green peppers, beans, lettuce, spinach, tomatoes, carrots, and more. It definitely requires a bit of an investment up front, but for them, it's already more than paid for itself in just the three years they've had it. The Oasis includes an automatic watering system, and Tara's husband installed a PVC pipeline from the house to the Oasis to avoid having an ugly hose stretched across the yard, so the garden saves them time as well.

Another popular option is square-foot gardening, where you build raised beds with one-foot-by-one-foot square plots (marked by strings or nylon lines) instead of in rows like traditional gardens. The idea is that you're able to use more of your garden space than you can with rows, and you aren't limited by poor soil conditions since the beds are raised and filled. A square-foot garden can be built on the ground or even on a table, and you can customize the beds to fit your space and needs.

Even if you don't have a yard, you can grow your own food. Urban gardening is gaining popularity with the rise of food costs and the growing emphasis on green living, and container gardens fit even on small balconies.

A stand-alone, raised bed, tabletop, or container garden protects delicate plants from animals and other pests that invade your yard, and requires very little weeding.

Harvesting

It's important to harvest the things you grow in your garden at their peak. This will vary for each fruit or veggie in your garden, so be sure to keep the seed packets or the cards that came with your seedlings.

Because gardening takes time and money, it's a good idea to have a plan for your harvest even before it starts producing so that it doesn't go to waste. You should, of course, use it, but you can also store it, freeze or can it, share it, or trade it!

Preserving Produce for the Winter

STORE IN A DARK, COOL PLACE:
- potatoes
- winter squash
- apples

BLANCH AND FREEZE:
- green beans
- broccoli
- peppers
- peas
- other greens

CAN:
- tomatoes
- cucumbers
- fruit
- green beans
- peas
- beets
- asparagus
- broccoli
- cauliflower

DRY:
- herbs
- fruits
- berries

Pest Control

One of the benefits of a home garden is avoiding the pesticides that most conventional farmers use. Organic produce is expensive, but growing it organically at home is actually less expensive since there aren't any chemicals to buy. It's not that you won't have pests when growing your own vegetables, but as long as you have a plan for dealing with them, it's not as hard to keep them away as you might think. The easiest way to deter pests is to include plants that deter pests. Gardens-Ablaze.com has a full list of companion plants for pest control (http://allingoodtime.net/companionplanting). Another easy way to control pests is to attract "good" bugs such as praying mantises and ladybugs to your garden. You can even hatch your own with a kit from Insect Lore, which Mandi and her girls enjoy doing each spring!

As you're cultivating your garden, watch for bugs and simply kill them by hand (or by shoe if, like us, you're not a huge fan of bugs) before they become a problem. If you're still dealing with pests, there are plenty of organic pesticides you can make at home from garlic, hot peppers, marigolds, chamomile, and more (http://allingoodtime.net/pesticides). For larger pests, such as deer, try a mechanical motion-activated Scarecrow sprinkler (http://allingoodtime.net/scarecrow).

Gardening Tips

J. D. Roth, the blogger behind GetRichSlowly.org and the author of *Your Money: The Missing Manual* (http://allingoodtime .net/yourmoney) has been documenting his experiences growing his own food for the past several years, including breakdowns of the costs and savings as well as tips for making the most of your garden and your harvest. He and his wife share these tips for beginning gardeners:

- Start planning your garden in February rather than waiting until it's time to start putting plants in the ground.
- Plant the things you'll actually eat. If your family doesn't eat a ton of zucchini, skip the zucchini and plant something you love!
- Do your research. Figure out what type of soil you have, where the sun shines and for how long, and what grows best in your area so that you can choose the right place for your

garden and add fill dirt or adjust the PH of your soil as necessary.

- Talk to other gardeners in your area to learn from their successes and failures. Form relationships and share seeds and seedlings to reduce everybody's costs.
- Be realistic about the up-front costs. While you'll save money in the long term, it's not cheap to start.
- Also be realistic about the time involved. You should be willing to invest fifteen to thirty minutes a day to maintaining your garden.
- Start small. It's tempting to go all out your first year, but take it a little at a time so that you don't get overwhelmed.

GRILLS

Tara's family can be found grilling as long as the grill isn't covered in snow (and when it is, they use a contact grill indoors!). One of their favorite quick meals is grilled chicken breasts with a side of grilled peppers and onions, along with a rice side that Tara can quickly prepare while her husband mans the grill.

TIP: Purchase larger packages of chicken breasts at the supermarket. Divide them up into large plastic freezer Ziploc bags, add your marinade, and freeze. Move them from the freezer to fridge the evening before, and you'll be ready to grill at the end of a busy day.

You'll start seeing sales on grills as early as August, when summer gear goes on sale, and those will increase after Labor Day, the last big "grilling out" holiday. By November and December, you should be able to pick up a grill at a deep discount, but by then your selection will be much more limited as well.

When buying a new grill, you first have to decide whether you want a gas or charcoal grill. Gas grills are generally easier to use, cook on, and clean up. They burn cleaner, there's no leftover ash, and you can control the temperature much more accurately. On the other hand, charcoal grills are less expensive and add a smoky flavor to food. They also fit better in small spaces and offer more portability. Although gas grills are generally more expensive up front, you'll spend much less on propane over the years than you will on charcoal and lighter fluid. However, there are rebates and coupons available on both fuel sources to cut your costs as well.

Gas Grills

When purchasing a gas grill, think carefully about how you plan to use it and what your total budget is for the grill as well as accessories. If you can, opt for porcelain-coated cast-iron or stainless-steel grates that heat evenly for the best cooking. Do you want the flexibility to prepare your entire meal on the grill? If so, look for grills with warming racks, side burners, and extra work space for chopping and preparing your food.

TIP: Be sure to budget for a propane tank, cover, wire brush, and basic grilling tools. Avid barbecuers may also want to invest in fake briquettes, wire boxes for grilling fish and veggies, and additional grill tools.

Charcoal Grills

When purchasing a charcoal grill, the list of features to look for is a little bit different. Although these grills are smaller, three hundred square inches of cooking space is a good place to start, which will allow you to grill six burgers and six hot dogs at a time. For better cooking, look for hinged cooking grates that you can raise to add more charcoal while grilling as well as vents both above and below the grate to help you achieve the perfect temperature. Because cleanup is harder with charcoal grills, you'll want to be sure to buy one that has a slide-out tray to easily remove the ash. You'll want to get a cover and grilling tools for your grill, and you may also invest in a chimney starter, which allows you to get your charcoal lit without the use of toxic lighter fluid.

INSECT REPELLENT

Mosquito and tick bites are not only uncomfortable, but they also carry the risk of serious disease and should be avoided whenever possible. However, as we've researched the effects of chemicals on the body—especially our kids' bodies—we're also hesitant to use DEET-based insect repellents.

Instead, look for things like citronella candles and rosemary sprays. Mandi's family really likes the Bug Bar from MadeOn, but to save money, you can actually make your own natural repellents. GardenMandy.com suggests dabbing vanilla extract or rubbing a lavender flower behind your ears and on your wrists to keep mosquitoes and other pests away.

TIP: Need to apply both sunscreen and insect repellent? Apply your sunscreen first and then apply the insect repellent so that the sunblock or sunscreen is the first layer on your skin and the scent of the insect repellent is on top.

Proper Tick Removal

Mandi lives in the boonies where ticks are an everyday occurrence during the warmer months. Rather than keeping their kids sequestered inside the house, she and her husband simply give the kids full-body tick checks twice a day and follow the recommended guidelines for safely removing any ticks that have bitten into the skin.

It's important that ticks be removed carefully and as soon as possible. Squeezing the body of the tick can actually cause its poison to be injected into the skin, as can separating the body from the head, and the longer a tick stays attached, the more likely it is to spread disease.

To remove a tick safely, grasp it with angled tweezers as close to the skin as possible and pull straight out. For ticks that are deeply embedded, you may want to have your family physician do it for you. If you're concerned about the length of time that the tick has been attached or have any other reason to suspect Lyme disease, you should save the tick in a plastic container or zippered bag and talk to your doctor about having it tested.

LANDSCAPING

To save on landscaping for your yard, buy shrubs and trees in the fall when garden centers are anxious to get rid of overstock before winter. Since the best time to plant them is actually in the fall anyway, this is a win-win. You can also buy bulbs at a discount in the fall and store them in a cool, dry space through the winter to plant in the spring.

LAWN CARE

Lawn care is something most people either love or hate, and we're both thankful that our husbands enjoy it because we sure don't!

Lawn Mowers

Lawn mowers generally go on sale after Labor Day with rock-bottom prices appearing in late October to November. The best time to mow your lawn is late in the day so that it has time to rest overnight before facing the harsh sun. To keep your lawn healthy, mow more often so that you don't have to cut as much off each time, which can damage the grass. You should also cut it at a higher setting, which helps with weed control.

Fertilizer

According to GardenGuides.com, coffee grounds make a great natural and inexpensive fertilizer. Save your own grounds or ask your favorite café or coffee shop if they have any to give away. You can also make your own compost from vegetable peelings and grass clippings.

Whether you're using a natural or a commercial fertilizer, you should fertilize in the spring and in the fall, although the exact schedule depends on the type of grass in your yard. See the sidebar for the exact schedule for various grasses. You'll also save time by leaving your grass clippings on your lawn when you mow so that they can provide a natural compost that will ultimately result in healthier grass with less fertilizing.

Lawn Fertilization Schedule (LawnCareGuide.com)

WARM GRASSES (BERMUDA, ZOYSIA, BAHIA, ST. AUGUSTINE):
- early spring: heavy application
- late summer: light application

COOL GRASSES (FESCUE, RYE GRASS, BLUEGRASS):
- early fall: heavy application
- late spring: light application

Watering the Lawn

The best time to water your lawn is in the early morning—the earlier the better—and if you live in an area where your lawn needs to be watered regularly, it may be worth investing in an automatic sprinkler system to save time (and sleep!).

MOTORCYCLES

Mandi's husband has owned both sport bikes and cruisers in the time that she's known him, although neither is very practical these days since they almost always have their kids with them. For a larger selection to choose from, the best time to buy a motorcycle is in the early spring; however, if you're looking for the lowest price, you'll want to buy in the off-season, particularly if you live in a colder climate that gets snow. You'll likely have to wait several months to take it for a spin if you buy in the winter, but the savings may be worth the delayed gratification.

When calculating the cost of a motorcycle, keep all of the associated expenses in mind, including licensing, taxes, helmets and other protective gear, and storage. Dealers will often include many of these items as part of a package deal, so make a point of asking about this when you're negotiating. Even if your state doesn't require you to wear a helmet, we recommend always wearing one. Is it really worth the risk of not protecting yourself?

OUTDOOR GEAR

Spring Gear

Umbrellas, raincoats, and rain boots usually make an appearance in late winter or early spring. These aren't often clearanced, so the best time to shop is in the early spring, when stores have the largest selection.

Summer Gear

Discounts appear after the Fourth of July. Hold out for a few weeks, and you'll be able to snag pool gear, swimwear, and sand toys at 50 percent off or more. You'll find the best prices in August and September, but your selection will be limited, especially for children's swimwear.

TIP: Rather than keeping your seasonal gear in their "proper" places—bathing suits with clothes, sunscreen in the bathroom, etc.—consider using a basket or bin to store all of it in a single location where it's easy to find and easy to get to. Whether your favorite destination is the pool, the park, the library, or your backyard, keeping everything you need in one place makes it easier to get out the door quickly without searching for the things you need.

Winter Outerwear

Starting in September you'll see winter gear in stores and a sale or two accompanying them. You'll see additional sales toward the end of the year, or you can wait until January or February to purchase at the very lowest prices. Just keep in mind that you may find that the selection is less than stellar by the end of the season. Purchase somewhere in between to find the best balance of price and choice of styles and colors.

Wrist Protectors for the Winter

To prevent snow from making its way between the end of coat sleeves and the top of gloves or mittens, take an old dress sock and cut a thumb hole in the heel. For little kids, the sock can be worn like a mitten, but for older kids and adults, you'll need to cut the end off to make room for their fingers to extend fully. Then put the sock on like a glove with the end tucked inside your long-sleeved shirt and coat for an extra layer of protection on your wrist.

TIP: With nine kids between us, we've both spent our fair share of time searching for rogue gloves and missing hats. To organize your winter gear, hang a shoe organizer on the back of the closet door or a sweater organizer from a main closet bar, assigning each child a specific section, so that the hats, gloves, and earmuffs are easy to find.

OUTDOOR TOYS

Parents are eager to buy play sets as soon as the weather turns nice, but waiting a month or so will net you a much nicer set at a big savings. Wait until August and you'll save even more. For durability and safety, we both recommend the wooden play sets over metal and plastic ones.

The best way to ensure that your playground equipment lasts is to regularly refinish and care for it. Replace missing or loose screws or nails and repair cracks yearly. You may also want to clean out and replace the sand yearly as well. Sanding and refinishing the whole playground should be done every couple of years, as necessary, in order to keep the wood healthy and prevent splitting and cracking.

It's important to use tubs or storage containers with drainage holes for outdoor toys to prevent them from sitting in stagnant water. Using a container with a lid will also cut down on sun damage when they're not in use. For easy and inexpensive outdoor toy storage, drill holes in the bottom of a plastic bin or rolling trash can, or use something like a mesh laundry bin or empty milk crate that already has plenty of holes.

Homemade Bubbles

Rather than spending a ton of money on bubbles (which inevitably get spilled or dumped out!), make your own at home by mixing the following ingredients:

1 cup water
4 tablespoons dishwashing liquid
2 tablespoons light Karo syrup or glycerin

PATIO FURNITURE

Prices on patio furniture will start inching down after July 4. Look for quality pieces that have removable and replaceable cushions in order to get the most for your money. If you're willing to be patient, watch Craigslist or local yard sales for gently used patio furniture rather than purchasing it new.

Because outdoor furniture is subject to all of the elements—heat, moisture, and/or cold—it's important to take care of it to make it last. Keep patio furniture clean and remove rust yearly. Cover furniture during the off seasons to protect it from the sun and moisture, or store cushions inside and away from the elements. Treat furniture with weather-resistant paints, varnishes, and/or stains to protect it year-round.

SHEDS

The best time to buy a shed is in the fall, more specifically in October, when sellers are trying to move inventory before the winter weather hits.

SPORTS ACTIVITIES & GEAR

When considering a starter sport for your kids, be sure to consider the long-term costs of various leagues. Ice hockey, football, figure skating, and golf are among the most expensive, while baseball/softball, basketball, flag football, soccer, and cross-country are the least expensive. Public, recreational, and church leagues are a fantastic way to give your kids the opportunity to try out various sports at a low cost before investing in more expensive private lessons or competitive leagues.

TIP: Many sports leagues open registration several months before the season. It's worth investigating early so that you can sign up for notifications or add a reminder to your calendar.

TIP: Set up a Google calendar to keep track of every family member's schedule. Tara and Luke typically allow their children to participate in only one sport at a time, but it still gets tricky when they all have different schedules. To maintain their sanity, they've created a shared family calendar via Google. At the beginning of each season, Tara adds all known practices, games, photo dates, etc. to the calendar. It then automatically syncs to her iPhone, as well as her husband's, so

As a kid and teen, Tara dabbled in soccer, basketball, and softball as well as cheerleading and rugby. She and her husband encourage their kids to participate in an organized sport or athletic activity each season, but their kids are allowed to choose the sport, with the understanding that they can't quit midseason. Their main goal is for their children to remain active and develop good sportsmanship, so they don't pressure them to stick with one sport season after season or to do a specific one if they're not interested in it.

they both know the schedules well in advance and can make plans accordingly.

Gear

Sports gear can be expensive, so it's important to start by prioritizing between needs and wants. Many leagues provide basic equipment, and this should be sufficient for the season. It's not necessary to have top-of-the-line equipment at the recreational level (or even at most other levels). If you're looking to purchase new gear, be sure to ask your local sports shop if they offer a group discount, and check your Sunday paper for coupons as well.

You'll find some sales during each sport's season, but the biggest discounts will be found as things are clearanced to make way for the next sport. You may also want to consider purchasing used, especially when it comes to kids' items that see little hard use. You'll find great used prices in the spring when people are likely to be purging and decluttering, so watch garage sales and consignment shops to pick up gently used gear.

SUN PROTECTION

Sunscreen sales start popping up as early as late April. Although drugstore prices are typically the highest, you'll find the best prices at these same stores when you pair a coupon with their loyalty programs. Follow the drugstore sales at Deal Seeking Mom for the best weekly deals (http://allingoodtime .net/drugstores).

Although we recommend stocking up on many household products, sunscreen is not one of them. With a shelf life of about a year, the risk isn't worth the money you might save! However, sun block has a longer shelf life and can be stockpiled. Mandi's family only uses sunblock because of some of the health risks associated with sunscreen. Read more about the differences between sunscreen and sun block at Life . . . Your Way (http://allingoodtime.net/sunscreen).

Application

Going to the beach with small children can be a lot of fun . . . or not. In many ways, getting ready for the sun and surf is akin to getting ready for playing in the snow, only the necessary gear is tight bathing suits and sunscreen instead of layers of snow clothes and boots. If at all possible, we recommend putting on sunscreen *before* you head out to the ocean so you can avoid rubbing your little one's skin raw with the inevitable pieces of sand that end up in your lotion or on their bodies.

Even when you're heading to your local park or pool, putting sunscreen on before you leave the house gives it time to work (did you know you're supposed to wait thirty minutes before going out in the sun?), and also prevents meltdowns by little ones who are anxious to play.

Although we both believe that sunshine can be good for us in the right circumstances, the beach or pool isn't the place to test that theory, and sun protection should be reapplied regularly and especially after swimming for the best protection.

TIP: Another option to simplify your beach trips and lazy days by the pool is to invest in sun-protective bathing suits, hats, and clothing. While you'll still need to apply sunscreen to exposed areas, applying sunscreen will take a lot less time. These can often be found for a steal on summer clearance racks, so buy a year ahead if your child's growth rate is fairly consistent.

SWIMMING POOLS

As with decks and other outdoor items, you'll find deals on swimming pool installation during the winter months in areas with four seasons. Contractors will also be less rushed, so your pool will actually get more attention. If you're determined to put in a pool during the summer, wait until after July 4, when contractors and suppliers start to offer deals on pool installation to entice customers who may be tempted to wait since the summer is halfway over anyway.

Before you build or purchase a pool, be sure to consider all of the costs and safety risks. Both of us are fairly paranoid about the dangers of a swimming pool with young children in the house. Mandi's family hopes one day to have a pool, but not until their youngest is at least eight years old. Make sure you properly fence your pool and add strong locks on the gate, not just to keep your own children out, but to keep other kids and animals out as well.

Pools, even the smaller aboveground ones, require a fair amount of maintenance, so you'll want to be prepared to purchase the necessary equipment and chemicals—or hire a pool-service professional to take care of those things for you.

You'll also need an insurance rider, so be sure to talk to your homeowner's insurance company ahead of time to get an estimate on those costs.

TOOLS

June is a popular month for sales on tools and power tools since these are common gifts for Father's Day. You'll also find deep discounts in November and December, particularly if you're willing to brave the crowds on Black Friday, as tools are often used as door busters to draw crowds to a store.

Ladders

While there's not a best time to purchase a ladder, do watch the sales. Craigslist can be a good resource for used ladders. Most experts agree that a hybrid fiberglass-and-aluminum ladder is worth the investment for quality and durability.

Seasonal Outdoor Projects

SPRING/SUMMER:
- Fertilize the lawn.
- Pressure-wash your siding.
- Inspect and clean decking and patios.
- Clear gutters and downspouts of debris.
- Inspect the attic for roof leaks.
- Patch cracks in driveways and sidewalks.
- Check foundation for cracks or deterioration.
- Trim vegetation and overgrown bushes.
- Clean your pool, checking chemical levels and adding water as necessary.
- Look for and remove wasp or hornet nests.
- Watch for signs of other pest problems.

FALL/WINTER:
- Clear gutters and downspouts of debris.
- Turn off outdoor spouts and remove hoses.
- Check and/or clean chimney.
- Winterize sprinkler system, pools, and ponds.
- Test your generator and check your gasoline supply.

Basement

ALARM SYSTEMS

Alarm systems provide peace of mind, and they also reduce the cost of your homeowner's insurance. To save money on your system, compare prices before choosing a company. Try different installation companies as well as different service providers and see which one offers the best deal.

When Mandi's family built their new home four years ago, they had an alarm system installed with a three-year service contract. A couple of years into the contract period, the company sent a notice that rates were increasing, but most contracts include a clause protecting you from rate changes during your contract period and instructions for opting out of your contract if they won't keep your plan at the initial rate, and they were able to keep their contracted rate. (It's a good idea to make sure this clause is included in any service contract you sign!)

DEHUMIDIFIERS

Just as dry air can cause problems during the winter, moist air can cause problems during the summer months, leading to soggy woodwork, stickiness, mustiness, and even mold. If you experience any of these signs of excess moisture, use a dehumidifier in your basement or other damp areas to reduce the humidity levels. You can typically find them on sale during the month of August.

TIP: If remembering to empty your dehumidifier is an issue, look for one that is equipped with a spout to attach a hose that can be directed to a floor drain.

DETECTORS

Look for deals on safety detectors such as smoke alarms and carbon-monoxide detectors in October, when safety is being highlighted during Fire Prevention Month. Parents may want to consider vocal smoke alarms since studies have shown that kids often sleep through the sound of regular detectors. These use vocal commands to wake up your children from a deep sleep in case you can't get to them, and although they are more expensive than traditional alarms, we think the peace of mind is worth the extra cost.

If you have an alarm system, consider having your detectors hardwired into it. Many insurance companies will offer a discount for having them continuously monitored, which should more than offset any additional charges by your alarm company.

TIP: Change the batteries in your detectors when you change the clocks for daylight savings, which is an easy way to make sure they get regular maintenance without having to add an extra reminder to your calendar. As an added bonus, you'll never have to worry about the alarm on the cathedral ceiling in your bedroom sounding the dreaded low-battery warning at three A.M.

HEATING & COOLING SYSTEMS

Common sense tells us that you'll get the best prices on fans and air conditioners during the winter months when the demand is the lowest. However, some stores may not stock the window/wall units or fans during the off-season. The opposite, of course, would be true for space heaters and kerosene heaters. Watch for sales at the very end of the proper season, and for smaller units, watch prices on Amazon.com and through other online retailers, because you may be able to get a better price online, especially through sites that offer free shipping.

Maintenance

Plan ahead for furnace or central air repairs and replacements rather than waiting until you have an emergency. You'll get quicker service, more attention, and better prices during the spring or fall when contractors are not tied up with emergency calls from extreme weather.

To maximize the efficiency of your a/c unit and furnace, be sure to clean them regularly. Change your furnace filter approximately every three months (more often when doing house projects that may create extra dust), and it's a good idea to check your cold-air return vents at this time as well to keep them clear.

A programmable thermostat will help you vary the temperatures when you're sleeping or away from home to save energy. Program it to turn your a/c up or your heat down during the day when you're away from home and to turn down your heat at night while you're sleeping.

TIP: During the summer, avoid using the oven as much as possible, opting to use the outdoor grill or Crock-Pot instead. You'll also want to keep your curtains closed on the windows that face the sun, since a surprising amount of heat can enter through even the most efficient window!

During the winter, be sure to check your door and window seals because drafts can make your heat much less efficient. Likewise, close vents and doors in rooms that you don't use regularly so that the air is directed more efficiently to the rooms that you do use. After baking in our ovens during the winter, we always leave the doors cracked so that the warm air can escape. Not only does this keep the fan from running to cool the oven down, but it also heats the kitchen. Likewise, open the curtains on the windows facing the sun to take advantage of the natural heat that comes through those windows. Since you lose a lot of heat through windowpanes when the sun's *not* shining, heavy drapes can also make your home warmer and more efficient in the winter.

During the winter, you'll use 3 to 5 percent less energy for every degree that you turn down your thermostat (when the lower temperature is sustained for at least five to six hours), so dress in layers, drink hot coffees, teas, and soups, wear slippers, use a space heater, and bake your meals to stay warm while reducing your power bill.

HOT-WATER TANKS

No matter what climate you live in, we can probably all agree that a hot-water heater is a blessing of modern life. We're thankful that we don't have to heat our bathwater on a stove (or over a fire!), and hot showers can be therapeutic and relaxing in addition to good hygiene.

Just as a programmable thermostat will help you reduce your heating and cooling costs, a water heater timer can help you reduce the energy used by your hot-water heater. Set it to turn off your water heater during periods when your family is not home or sleeping.

Improve the efficiency of your hot-water heater by wrapping it in an insulating blanket, which keeps heat from escaping through the outer walls and therefore reduces the energy used to keep your hot water hot. It might seem like a little thing, but the little things add up, and this is an inexpensive way to save money for years to come.

If you're looking to save even more on your hot-water

heater—and with six girls between us that will be teenagers all too soon, we both are—tankless water heaters can significantly reduce the cost of hot water because they heat water as needed rather than storing the hot water in the tank. They do require an up-front investment, but if you're looking to replace your hot-water heater anyway, be sure to consider a tankless one.

TIP: If you have young children in your home, it's important to keep your hot-water heater turned down to 120 to 125 degrees to reduce the chances of serious burns. Mandi's grandparents keep their hot-water heater set at the highest temperature, and when Mandi visits them, she's always surprised by just how hot the water gets when it's accidentally turned on full force.

Maintenance

In order to keep your hot-water tank running at peak efficiency, clean it regularly to clear out any sediment that has built up at the bottom. How often you need to do this depends on your water supply and how quickly the sediment builds up, and the only way to figure it out is to drain it and then check it again every six months. If you don't find much sediment the first few times you do it, you probably only need to flush it every two to three years.

Energy Tax Credits

Reducing the energy your home uses not only reduces your electric bill but many of those costs also qualify for residential energy credits on your taxes, so you can recoup some of the cost of making your home more efficient.

QUALIFYING EXPENSES INCLUDE (IRS FORM 5695):
- Insulation material or system designed to reduce heat loss or gain
- Exterior windows, doors, and skylights
- Metal roofing with pigmented coatings or asphalt roofing with cooling granules that meet Energy Star requirements
- Certain natural gas, propane, or oil furnaces and hot-water boilers
- Certain electric heat pumps, central air conditioners, water heaters, and biomass heating units
- Certain solar, wind, and geothermal units
- Certain main air circulating fans used in oil furnaces

HUMIDIFIERS

Adding a whole-house humidifier to your furnace will prevent the air from becoming too dry during the winter months, which can lead to dry skin, static, sore throats, and more susceptibility to illness as well as damage to your home. The humidifier runs only when the heater does, and since the heater is the cause of the dry air, you're not wasting energy by running it too often.

Single-room humidifiers are a good investment for use when a whole-house humidifier isn't feasible. We recommend you choose a cool-mist humidifier versus a warm-mist one. They're both equally effective, but cool-mist humidifiers tend to be less expensive and are safer for use around small children. Wipe down your single-room humidifier daily with a 10 percent bleach solution to safely keep it clean.

LAUNDRY

Appliances

New washer and dryer models are typically released in September and October, making this the ideal time to find bargain pricing as stores try to move older models to make room for the new inventory. You'll also find significant discounts on just about any holiday weekend when stores price these lower to draw in additional customers during a typically slow period. If you're having a hard time deciding whether you really *need* a new washer and/or dryer, keep in mind that a little planning is a good way to get a better price rather than waiting until your current model dies. You'll also get long-term cost savings with the high-efficiency units that are now available.

Maintenance

To keep your washer and dryer in top condition and extend their lives, be sure to do regular preventive maintenance. This means clearing the lint trap with every load of laundry you dry, as well as checking and cleaning the hoses and ductwork every six to twelve months. High-efficiency washers have such a tight seal that they can grow mildew in the drum over time. To prevent this, leave the door open for several hours after each load you run. You may need to modify your laundry routine or make sure you can lock the door to your laundry room if you have little ones who may be tempted to climb inside the washer if they find the door left standing open!

Laundry Products

Laundry products are frequently on sale, so if you're brand loyal, clip those coupons and hold on to them to purchase several bottles at once when they're at their lowest price. Keep in mind that the biggest savings will not always be the largest bottle available when you have a coupon, so compare the unit pricing carefully. We consider 10 cents an ounce to be the stock-up price if you're looking for the best deal available.

Most of us use far too much detergent or fabric softener in a single load because we just fill the cup up to the top. Use a black Sharpie to make the guide lines in the cup stand out, but even then you can use less than the recommended amount in each load. Similarly, you can cut dryer sheets in half to double the number of loads you get out of a box.

To save money on the water and electricity needed to run your washer and dryer, use cold water for all of your loads, even whites. The regular cycle is usually enough to get clothes clean unless they are very dirty, in which case you may want to run a longer cycle or do a double rinse. Some areas charge higher electrical rates during peak hours, so you can save money by running things like the washer and dryer at night.

During the summer, you'll also put less strain on your air-conditioning unit by running these heat-generating appliances at night when it's cooler outside.

One of the ways that Mandi stays on top of laundry at her house is by folding clothes right out of the dryer. Loads seem to multiply once they're taken out of the dryer and put in a laundry basket, so she tries to get them folded right away. Putting them away, though, is another story!

If you're looking for green and frugal alternatives to traditional laundry detergent, try making your own detergent (see sidebar) or using soap nuts, the berrylike fruit of the Sapindus mukorrosi tree, found mainly in the Himalayas. The berries are gathered, their seeds are removed, and they're dried in the sun. Because they're grown organically and then dried, they really are 100 percent natural. They're also gentle, biodegradable, antimicrobial, and low-sudsing, making them safe for high-efficiency washers. We like Laundry Tree brand soap nuts.

Homemade Laundry Detergent

While there are recipes available for both liquid and powdered laundry detergents, Alyssa from KingdomFirstMom.com prefers this powdered recipe because it's much faster and easier, both to prepare and to use:

YOU'LL NEED:
  1 bar of Zote (14 oz.)
  1 bar of Fels-Naptha (5 oz.)

4 cups Borax

4 cups washing soda (NOT baking soda)

Slice each of the bars into three to four pieces and either hand-grate them or run them through a food processor until finely ground. Then combine all four ingredients in a large, sturdy container with a lid, and you're ready to go!

DRY CLEANING

One of the best ways to save money on dry cleaning is to use at-home dry-cleaning kits or hand-launder with Woolite. How do you know if you can safely launder an item at home? If an item is simply marked "dry clean," gentle cleaning at home is a safe alternative. However, if an item is marked "dry clean only," a trip to the dry cleaners is necessary. If you do need to take your clothes to the dry cleaners, wear things like suit jackets and pants several times before taking them. Watch for coupons and special offers in home mailers as well.

Frugal Stain Removers

The key to removing any stain is to not put the stained garment in the dryer until all traces of the stain have been removed since a dryer can permanently set the stain. For everyday stains, rubbing a bit of laundry detergent on the spot before washing the item is often enough. Vinegar and sunlight both serve as excellent stain removers on their own as well. For more serious stains, try these:

BABY POOP, SPIT-UP:
Soak clothes overnight in a tub with one cup dishwasher soap and one cup color-safe powdered bleach.

BLOOD:
Rinse immediately with cold water; for older stains, treat with hydrogen peroxide.

FOOD DYE (JUICE, POPSICLES, ETC.):
Soak the stain in rubbing alcohol and then wash as usual.

GRASS:
Blot the stain with vinegar; for tougher stains, mix vinegar and baking soda and brush stain with an old hairbrush.

GUM:
Stick clothing in the freezer to harden the gum; for larger items, apply ice.

INK/MARKERS:
Blot the stain with a rag or cotton ball soaked in rubbing alcohol until the ink stops running or spray the stain with hair spray and blot with a Q-tip.

LIPSTICK:
Spray the stain with hair spray and let sit; use a clean, damp white cloth to blot the stain.

OIL:
Apply a paste made of cornstarch and water and let dry before washing.

RUST:
Rub with vinegar and salt before washing.

WINE, COFFEE, FRUIT:
Soak in regular white vinegar or club soda.

IRONING

Ironing is not our favorite household chore, so we both do our best to avoid it! To reduce the need for ironing, pull clothes out of the dryer while they're still warm. Also look for clothes that don't need a lot of ironing. Little-girl dresses with ruffles on the front often get wrinkled and misshapen, as do thin cotton-collared shirts. That's okay for special occasions, but save time by avoiding these items for everyday clothing.

If you have an ironing board with a particleboard or wood surface, put a layer of foil underneath the padding. The foil will conduct the heat and reduce the amount of time you spend ironing!

LINE DRYING

Reduce your energy usage and cut your electricity bill significantly by hanging your clothes to dry—outside or inside—rather than tossing them in the dryer. There's also something relaxing about standing in the sunshine and hanging your clothes, although it definitely takes more time than tossing them in the dryer!

While the dryer actually wears away fabrics (that's where all the lint comes from!), the clothesline can help clothes last longer. However, avoid hanging most things in the harsh midday sun since that can cause them to fade and wear out. To reduce fading, hang clothes inside out, and hang them upside down to prevent stretching. If you dislike the stiffness that comes from line drying, you can always toss the load into the dryer for a few minutes once they're dry. Be sure not to hang knits and other items that say "lay flat to dry" on the label because they can become misshapen, and unmentionables should be air-dried inside rather than in the sun to preserve their elasticity.

If you live in a development, one caveat to keep in mind before hanging a laundry line outside is to check with your homeowner's association about any guidelines. Unfortunately, many prohibit clotheslines, as they're considered an eyesore.

Alternatives to Fabric Softeners & Dryer Sheets

Both fabric softeners and dryer sheets work by adding a thin layer of chemicals to your clothing to make them feel soft and prevent static electricity. Unfortunately, many of these chemicals are actually toxic, so if you're looking for a healthier alternative, try these:

- Add one-half cup of baking soda to your washer before adding your clothes.
- Add a cup of vinegar to your washer before adding your clothes. The effectiveness of both these methods depends on your water type, so you may want to try one and then the other to see which works best for you.
- Add a tennis ball to the dryer to help loosen fibers as they dry (of course, many people say that this is no better, since heating rubber can lead to off-gassing of chemicals).
- Andrea Dekker from SimpleOrganizedLiving.com pins a couple safety pins to items in each load to cut down on static buildup.

Or just skip it all. Mandi and her family have never used dryer sheets or fabric softeners, and they don't notice too many issues with stiff clothing or static cling.

SEPTIC SYSTEMS

Septic systems are installed when a house is built or when it needs to be replaced, so there's not really a "best" time to purchase one, but you can certainly save down the road if you are careful about the things that you put down your drains. When Mandi's family built their home in rural West Virginia, they didn't even install a garbage disposal—which is pretty much a standard convenience in most homes these days—because kitchen waste can quickly fill and clog a septic system. Likewise, feminine products shouldn't be flushed because they can fill a septic system quickly.

In order to reduce how often you need to empty your tank, avoid heavy-duty cleaners, grease, and hazardous chemicals, which all break down the healthy bacteria in your septic system as well as the drain field itself. Most experts advise having the tank pumped every two to three years to keep it working at its peak. A septic system can be pumped at any time of the year, although the warm ground during the spring and summer helps the healthy bacteria in your septic system to start up more quickly after it's been pumped, so the warmer months may be better.

STORAGE CONTAINERS

January is a great time to watch for sales and discounts on storage containers, since many people resolve to get organized at the start of the New Year. However, any professional organizer will tell you that you should never buy containers until you know exactly what you're going to do with them. First declutter and sort through your stuff and *then*—once you know what you want to keep and how you want to organize it—purchase the appropriate containers.

Plastic bins are the most popular storage containers because they're inexpensive and protect the contents from moisture. The one drawback is that they can hold moisture in, causing water damage or mold growth if damp items are stored inside, so you'll want to make sure that you don't pack anything away that is moist. Cardboard boxes are also popular because you can pick them up for free from grocery stores and liquor stores. However, you run the risk of water damage, especially if your boxes are stored in the basement. Important documents and precious mementos should be stored in a fire-safe box rather than in traditional storage containers, although you'll have to choose these carefully because fire safes can be expensive and offer a limited amount of space. IKEA is an inexpensive source for colorful cardboard containers if appearances are important.

TIP: Rather than just tossing boxes into the basement and calling it storage, organize your boxes so that your storage is actually functional and you can find what you're looking for when you need to. Group boxes of similar items—clothes, books, seasonal decor—so that they're all together. You may even want to use different-colored boxes, such as the red and green ones that are available at Christmastime, to differentiate between the different groups. On the outside of *every* box include a broad description of the contents in big letters, for example CHRISTMAS, followed by a smaller detailed description of what's inside—*ornaments, stockings, and tree topper.*

STORM WINDOWS

The best way to improve the performance of old windows is to replace them with newer windows that are more energy efficient. However, a less expensive alternative is to buy storm windows, especially if you can plan ahead and buy them in the spring or summer before the higher-demand months.

Storm windows should be installed in October before the cold weather hits and taken down in April before the hot weather arrives to provide the most benefit. Always inspect your storm windows for broken seals and panes, loose corner joints, and to make sure that they form a tight seal with the window.

SUMP PUMPS

A sump pump is used in basements with bathrooms or kitchenettes to pump drain water up to the main draining system as well as to prevent flooding in basements that are below the water table level. If you live in an area that is prone to flooding, you might also consider installing a backup pump, especially if your basement is finished. This is one area where you'll want to invest in a high-quality pump if you can. Tara's home was built in 2004, and the builders installed a lower-quality pump that has failed twice over the years. They've since upgraded to one with a lifetime warranty and also added an inexpensive water alarm that's powered by a nine-volt battery that will alert them at the first sign of water on the floor.

UTILITY BILLS

Although it can feel like utilities are the one bill you're stuck with no matter what, there are ways to lower your monthly bills. Even though some of them may seem small, the savings add up:

Electricity

- Reduce electricity usage by bumping your thermostat higher in the summer and lowering it in the winter, as mentioned in the previous section.

- If your home is anything like ours, you have gadgets on top of gadgets. Rather than plugging all of your electronics directly into the wall, plug them into power strips and switch them off when not in use to reduce the vampire power usage.

- Use CFL bulbs in place of traditional incandescent bulbs in all lighting fixtures to reduce energy consumption. Or better yet, consider investing in LED lightbulbs. They are priced significantly higher, but they can last twenty years or more and have none of the associated risks of mercury contamination that go hand in hand with CFL bulbs. Also encouraging household members to turn off lights in rooms that aren't being used and utilizing timers can save on the costs of electricity associated with lighting your home.

- Many utility companies charge higher rates for usage during peak times, usually noon to 7 P.M. Plan your laundry and dishwashing schedule for early morning and late evening in order to save.

- To make it easier to budget, ask your utility company about a fixed bill plan that averages your power usage over twelve months so that you pay a set amount each month rather than dealing with fluctuations between twenty-degree and seventy-degree days.

Water

- Newer toilets use only about 1.5 gallons to flush. However, if your toilet was installed prior to 1995, you may benefit from placing a brick or jug of water in the tank to reduce the amount of water used per flush. For stay-at-home parents and families with several children, saving a gallon or two of water with every flush can quickly add up!

- Avoid wasting water when running the tap for cold or hot water by collecting the waste in jugs that can be stored as an emergency water supply or used to water indoor plants or your garden.

- Use energy-efficient showerheads to significantly cut down the amount of water that you use in the shower.

- Only run your dishwasher or washing machine with full loads because they use close to the same amount of water regardless of how much is in them. If you have a newer model, washing dishes in the dishwasher rather than by hand will actually save water and energy.

- Turn off the water while brushing your teeth, and teach your children to do the same.

Cable, Internet, Phone

- To save money on your cable, phone, and Internet bills, look for communications companies that combine all three, which is the best way to save on monthly expenses.

- Alternatively, many families these days are choosing to cancel their landline numbers in favor of cell phones since most people carry their cell phones with them all of the time anyway. If you opt to keep your landline, scale back to the basic service. Consider dropping features such as caller ID, and screen calls with your voice mail instead.

- These days, there are so many ways to save on long-distance calls that it doesn't really need to be an issue for most budgets. The two best ways to stay in touch with friends and family across the country—and even internationally—are by using your cell phone (especially if you have free nights and weekends on your plan) and using Skype. Skype allows you to video-chat with other users, or you can set up an inexpensive plan to be able to call landlines and cell phones as well. Tara and her husband use their cell phones for all of their long-distance calls!

- Because Mandi and her family live in a rural area where cell coverage can be spotty, they use a third-party service, OneSuite.com, which offers long distance for just 2.5 cents per minute. You can also find long-distance calling cards at warehouse stores. For example, at the time we're writing this, Costco offers a seven-hundred-minute prepaid card for just 2.86 cents per minute.

- You can also scale back your cable and Internet plans, opting for fewer "premium" channels and slower Internet.

TIP: Our number one suggestion for reducing these costs is to simply ask. Ask your utility providers if they'll discount your bill if you set up automatic payments. If they won't, shop around to see what other providers are charging because you may be able to get a lower rate somewhere else. Be sure to reevaluate your options on a yearly basis to ensure that you're receiving a fair price.

Customer-service call centers are typically busier in the mornings and at the beginning of the week, so try to call in the midafternoon in the middle of the week to get the best service.

WATER TREATMENT SYSTEMS

Whether your water contains naturally occurring minerals and deposits through a well system or you're worried about hormones and other additives in city water, a whole-house water treatment system is a good way to reduce drinking water and clothing replacement costs.

First, find out if you really need a whole-house system. Lowe's and other home maintenance stores sell water testing kits, or your local well company may do it for free. If your water comes back positive for chlorine, chloroform, pesticides, or organic chemicals, you may need a carbon filter. If your water contains sodium, ferrous iron, nitrates, lead, fluoride, or organic contaminants, a reverse osmosis system may be a better option, but these systems also waste a lot of water, so don't install one if it's not necessary.

TIP: If you'd simply like to purify your drinking and cooking water, consider investing in a ZeroWater treatment system (http://allingoodtime.net/zerowater). They're proven to reduce total dissolved particles to 000 parts per million for a reasonable cost.

WINTER WEATHER

In general, you'll want to make sure you have your snow removal items ready to go *before* winter hits. The best way to get these at a discount is to pick up whatever you need as the items go on sale in late February so that you'll be ready for the following year. Stores in our areas often run out of these items when a winter storm warning is issued, so while it may be tempting to wait until you need them to buy them, you may be stuck without a shovel if you do.

While Mandi's family now has gravel pathways and a gravel driveway that doesn't need to be salted or sanded, we recommend salting or sanding at the beginning of a snowfall and again after you clear away a heavy fall. If you're expecting an ice storm, you'll want to salt before it hits *unless* there's already snow on the ground, in which case it's best to leave the snow. Although it will be heavier to remove, the snow cushion reduces the risk of someone taking a spill and getting hurt.

Traditional rock salt is harmful to plants, pets, and other wildlife and contaminates water sources through runoff. Because it doesn't naturally break down, these effects on the environment are long-lasting. According to GreenLivingOnline .com, all deicers are made from chemicals, and so there is no truly "green" alternative. Your best bet is to use a mixture to prevent the buildup of any single chemical and to sweep up any that is left behind rather than letting it be washed away. Clearing your sidewalks and driveways with a snowblower also reduces the need for a deicer, and sand can also give you extra traction on a slick surface, although it's obviously more expensive than the chemical alternatives.

SPRING/SUMMER:
- Clean and reverse ceiling fans.
- Test smoke and carbon-monoxide detectors.

- Change furnace filter.
- Open windows to let fresh air in.
- Declutter.
- Switch seasonal wardrobes.
- Deep-clean your home.

FALL/WINTER:
- Clean your humidifier.
- Clean and reverse ceiling fans.
- Change furnace filter.
- Test smoke and carbon-monoxide detectors.
- Check weather stripping around doors and windows.
- Flush your water heater.
- Test smoke and carbon-monoxide detectors.
- Have your septic system pumped and/or inspected.
- Remove screens and install storm windows.
- Check propane/oil level.
- Open windows to let fresh air in.
- Switch seasonal wardrobes.

Bathroom

BATH TOYS

To save money on bath toys, just don't bother with them! Mandi's kids spend hours playing with cups, spoons, and other kitchen items in the bath or shower, so there's no reason to spend money on actual bath toys unless you want to.

TIP: No matter what type of toys you use, they can grow mildew over time, even if you're doing your best to dry them after use. Run them through the dishwasher regularly to keep them clean, and look for an organizer made of mesh or with plenty of drain holes in the bottom so that they don't sit in water when they're not in use.

CLEANING

Cleaning the bathroom isn't our favorite chore (is it anybody's?), but we have found a few tips and tricks along the way to make it easier and less expensive:

- Use baking soda and vinegar, which cut through grime and disinfect surfaces, for most of your bathroom cleaning. Use full-strength vinegar for toilets and grimy areas or dilute it in water for an everyday cleaner, and baking soda can be used as a scrub with water or vinegar.

- Be careful not to cross-contaminate the surfaces in your bathroom. We tend to use multiple rags for the different areas in the bathroom, but you could get away with using one if you start with benign surfaces such as shelves and then move to the sink and vanity and then the shower before doing your toilet. Once your rag or sponge touches the toilet, though, its next stop should always be the laundry room, not another surface in your bathroom!

- Wipe shower walls and doors with car wax every six months to protect them against water spots and stains.

- Skip all of the cleaners and opt for a steam cleaner instead, which can cost anywhere from $35 to $500. The steam cleans and disinfects, and you don't need any additional rags or cleaners, which reduces the amount you'll spend on cleaning supplies in the future.

- Keep cleaning supplies under your sink or in the linen closet so you can easily grab them for a quick clean. If

The Toilet Paper Principle

Toilet paper can be one of the most difficult items to stockpile. Even when it is on sale, it can be hard to figure out whether you're really getting a bargain on it. With double rolls and ultra packs, etc., how do you know if you're paying a reasonable price or not?

In general, 50 cents is a good price for a double roll. But if you want a more precise rule to follow, find the total square feet on the front of your toilet paper package. Move the decimal point two places to the left. That number represents a cost of 1 cent or less per square foot and gives you your "stock-up price."

For example:

- 400 sq. ft. = 4.00 when you move the decimal point, so the stock-up price is $4 for that size package.
- 650 sq. ft. = 6.50 when you move the decimal point, so the stock-up price is $6.50 for that size package.

your supplies are easy to grab, you can wipe your sink and vanity daily in under a minute, or clean the bathroom as Tara does while her kids play in the bathtub.

COSMETICS

Drugstores often put cosmetics on clearance in January to make room for the new colors and styles. This is also a great time to pick up leftover holiday gift sets at deep discounts.

To save money on cosmetics, watch for coupons that you can match with weekly deals at the drugstores (http://allin goodtime.net/drugstores). Although you may want to invest in higher-quality brands for the products you use every day, pick up trendy colors at drugstores first to see if you really like them. Tara's favorite lipstick is actually a $2.99 tube of cherry-flavored Nivea Lip Care. It adds just the right amount of color and keeps her lips from getting chapped in the colder months. We've also read that the only real difference between a high-end mascara and a "bargain" mascara is the brush, and you could easily save the brush from a more expensive product to use in your inexpensive formulation.

TIP: For longer-lasting makeup, wait at least ten minutes after applying moisturizer before you apply your foundation. Both of us use and prefer Bare Minerals makeup, but if you're using a cream foundation, it's also important to use a powder to set it. For longer-lasting eye makeup, choose waterproof varieties and stick with liquid eyeliners. Mandi brushes cornstarch over her eyelids to absorb any excess oil or moisture before applying eyeliner or shadow. For longer-lasting lipstick, apply foundation and lip liner before your color.

Brushes

Check out EyesLipsFace.com for quality makeup brushes that won't break your budget. It's amazing how much difference a good brush can make in the application of both budget and department-store cosmetics.

Experts recommend washing your makeup brushes every week to keep them clean and make them last longer. Likewise, most experts recommend replacing mascara every three months and other makeup every one to two years. We'll admit we don't always follow the recommendations. Oops!

HAIRCUTS

If you're looking to save money on haircuts, the obvious solution is to do it yourself at home. Mandi often cuts her four daughters' long hair (which leaves lots of room for error!) and she's been known to cut her own layered hair as well, but that doesn't always work out as expected. Tara's husband cuts his hair as well as their boys', which not only saves money but also time. Unfortunately, their daughters have also been known to cut their own hair, which saved neither time nor money, so be sure to keep those clippers and scissors well out of reach in between haircuts.

There are plenty of kits and videos available for learning to cut hair at home, and it may be worth attempting while your children are young—before they care as much about the way it looks—so that you have plenty of time to improve your skills.

We'll both continue cutting our kids' hair at home until they express an interest in having their hair done by a professional, and then we'll reconsider!

If your hair is a simple or basic style, try a local cosmetology school, where beauticians-in-training practice their skills under the watchful eyes of professionals. If you're not that brave, look for a professional who now works from home, cutting hair on the side, because their rates are likely to be significantly less than a salon's. But if only a salon will do, most have different levels for their stylists with a corresponding range of rates, so ask when making an appointment.

TIP: Daily deals sites, like Groupon and Eversave (http://allingoodtime.net/dailydeals), often have salon specials at 50 percent or more off retail. This is a great way to save on haircuts, especially when you want to go the extra mile for a special event.

Scheduling an appointment

As with most professional appointments, try to schedule your hair appointments first thing in the morning, before the crowd descends. During the day is always better than the late afternoons and evenings since you won't be competing with people who work during the day. If you're getting your hair cut for a special event, schedule your appointment for two weeks before the event to ensure that your hair has time to grow just a bit to avoid that just-got-a-haircut look!

TIP: If you use pomades, mousse, or gel regularly, it's a good idea to wash your hair with clarifying shampoo once every one to two weeks to get rid of any buildup from your styling products. For a frugal (and more gentle) alternative, add a couple teaspoons of baking soda and a few drops of lemon juice to your regular shampoo.

HEALTH & BEAUTY ITEMS

You might think that drugstores are overpriced—and in general this is true—but when you learn how to shop at them using their store loyalty programs, you can regularly purchase toothpaste, deodorant, shampoo, razors, and more at as much as 75 percent off retail or completely free! Yes, it sounds a little too good to be true, but it's completely legitimate and very easy to do.

Each drugstore chain has its own loyalty program, so we won't go into the specifics, but basically they offer sales items each week with store rewards that you can use on a future purchase. By purchasing these reward items with coupons, you can dramatically lower your out-of-pocket costs while earning rewards that you can apply as payment to a future purchase. When you do this regularly, you get into a cycle where you're continually paying for your purchases with these rewards while still earning more rewards. At Deal Seeking Mom, Tara regularly features the weekly deals at all three major drugstores—CVS, Walgreens, and Rite Aid—to help her readers find the best deals each week (http://allingoodtime.net/drugstores).

Another way to save on health-and-beauty items is to purchase trial-size products with regular coupons that make them deeply discounted or even free. If a coupon does not spe-

Homemade Foaming Hand Soap

Save money on hand soap by making your own foaming hand soap. As an added bonus, you can avoid products with triclosan, an antibacterial agent that is found in most antibacterial soaps and kills not only the bad bacteria but also the good bacteria and contributes to the growth of superbugs.

To get started, you'll need:

- foaming hand soap dispenser
- castile soap
- water, straight from the tap

Add one to two tablespoons of castile soap to the dispenser and then fill it with water. That's it!

Dr. Bronner's castile soap comes in a variety of natural scents, from peppermint to almond (Mandi's favorite), so you don't have to sacrifice the clean smell to save money!

cifically state what sizes it's good on, it is valid for use on trial and travel sizes. This is a great way to stock your diaper bag, gym bag, or get extras for your purse and traveling.

LINENS

January is the best time of year to purchase towels, which is a perfect way to freshen up you home. Many stores host white sales at this time of year with significant discounts on these items. You'll also find towels at discounted prices at overstock stores such as T.J.Maxx, Marshalls, and HomeGoods or at warehouse stores like Costco. Online, try Overstock.com.

High-quality towels have loops that stand up straight and tall. They're soft but they also have some weight to them, which shows that they're more absorbent. And of course, make sure you get towels that are big enough. The least expensive bath towels often barely wrap around your middle, while an over-size bath towel or bath sheet allows you to wrap yourself up fully and walk around without feeling exposed!

If you use a towel bar in your bathroom, fold your towels vertically so that you can simply drape them over the towel bar when you're ready to use them. See how Mandi's husband folds them at http://allingoodtime.net/linens.

MEDICAL CARE

Doctor's Appointments

With nine kids between us, it's hard to say how much time our families have wasted in waiting rooms over the past ten years! To avoid long waits, schedule appointments first thing in the morning or right after lunch, and when possible, avoid Mondays and Fridays for routine checkups.

Don't rule out the quick-service clinics that many drugstores and grocery stores now host. They offer trained professionals who have the ability to diagnose and write prescriptions and are covered under your standard copay. They're often far less crowded than regular doctor's offices and urgent-care clinics, offer extended hours, and no appointment is necessary. Plus you can fill any prescriptions immediately, making them a fast and simple option for minor illnesses.

TIP: Although pediatrician's offices often have toys and books to keep kids busy while waiting, we try to avoid using them since you're likely to leave with more germs than you came with! Instead, pack books or small toys in your diaper bag or purse or pull out your iPhone to keep the kids busy. Mandi's family collects the crayons that the kids get at restaurants and keeps them in the diaper bag, and the paper that covers the exam table makes a great surface for drawing or playing tic-tac-toe while you wait!

Payment

As with all health-care costs, always ask your doctor how you can decrease the expense of appointments and procedures that are not covered by insurance. Many offer cash discounts if you're willing to pay up front, and many providers also offer payment plans.

Eye Care

Many big-box retailers like Walmart have on-site eye-care centers where you can get an inexpensive exam and also purchase glasses and contacts. However, it's important to note that there's a difference between an optometrist (like those at Walmart) and an ophthalmologist, and it's a good idea to see an ophthalmologist—who is a trained M.D.—regularly since they are better trained to spot potential serious problems with your eyes.

Mandi and her husband, Sean, both wear contacts, and

their oldest daughter wears glasses. For contacts, they have been using 1-800 Contacts for years and have always been extremely happy with the prices and speed of delivery. Their favorite sources for discount glasses include Zenni Optical and Just Eyewear, where you can purchase prescription glasses online for as low as $8 a pair. Your prescription will have most of the information you need except for your measurements, but you can ask for that information at your visit or take the measurements yourself.

Flu Shots

As flu season approaches each year, drugstores, grocery stores, and doctor's offices often host flu shot clinics. Keep in mind that your time is valuable, and paying a few extra dollars may be worth the convenience of going to the one closest or most accessible to you, but if you have several options, watch for coupons that reduce the cost. Some of the big drugstores have even been known to offer fairly hefty in-store purchase coupons when you get your flu shot, which is a great way to pick up other household necessities for less.

The Centers for Disease Control and Prevention recommend getting the seasonal flu vaccine as soon as it's available in your community, and there doesn't seem to be any benefit to waiting as far as discounts or availability.

We've all heard the warnings and anecdotal stories about vaccines, and if your family wants to avoid the flu shot while still reducing your risk of illness, be sure to talk to your family physician about the role that vitamin D3 plays in a healthy immune system. A simple blood test can check your current vitamin-D levels so that each member of your family can be put on an appropriate dose. Some people choose to skip the testing and stick with the recommended dosing from vitamin manufacturers, but we recommend talking to your doctor first!

Alyssa from KingdomFirstMom.com also recommends these other ways to stay healthy during flu season without the flu shot:

- Get fifteen to twenty minutes of sunshine a day whenever possible (easier for those in warmer climates than for us!).

- In addition to vitamin D3, take a daily probiotic to improve your general health.

- Garlic is a cheap but effective way to fend off viruses. To take, cut a clove into small pieces and swallow it. You might smell like garlic for a couple days, but that's probably better than being sick!

Health Insurance

Rising health insurance costs are affecting many families, but there are things you can do to reduce your costs. As with any insurance, one of the most dramatic ways to reduce your monthly fees is to increase your copays and yearly deductible. If your family is relatively healthy and you have money in savings, this is a great option for reducing your monthly cost. In families where both spouses have insurance benefits, be sure to scrutinize both plans to see which plan offers the best coverage at the lowest cost. In some cases, it may even make sense to split your family's coverage between both plans.

Consider alternative plans as well. Mandi and her family are members of Samaritan Ministries, a health-care sharing ministry that actually splits the medical bills of members among other participants. Each month they send a "share" payment directly to another family to go toward their medical bills, and when they have medical needs, those amounts are assigned to other members as well. They've been members for more than four years, and during that time they've delivered a baby, dealt with serious medical issues with one of their daughters, and had more than one ER visit, all of which have been covered by the shares they've received from other members.

Many companies offer flexible spending accounts (FSA) as an employee benefit. With an FSA, you elect to deposit a certain amount of pretax money into your account at the beginning of the year, and you can then use that money for health-care needs such as doctor and dentist visits, eyeglasses, over-the-counter and prescription drugs, and more. You need to be careful not to overstate your needs because you'll lose any money that you haven't used by the end of the year, but these accounts are a great way to save on your out-of-pocket costs if you calculate the amount you'll need carefully.

Finally, don't discount the benefit of getting healthy. You'll save the most on health care if you don't need to use it, so focus on a healthy diet and exercise regimen for your entire family and look for natural ways to boost your immunity as well!

Mammograms & Breast Exams

An important part of women's health is regular breast exams, both self-checks at home and routine mammograms. The official recommendation by both the American Cancer Society and the National Cancer Institute is that women forty years and older should have a mammogram every one to two years. However, there are risks associated with mammograms (most of which are outweighed by the benefits), and you should discuss both with your doctor.

The National Breast Cancer Foundation recommends that all women twenty years or older do a breast self-exam at least once a month. With more than 70 percent of breast cancers discovered through self-exams and such clear correlations between early detection and survival, this is worth marking on your calendar. Consider making it part of your monthly routine—perhaps after your monthly menstrual cycle or on the same day that you sit down to pay bills—so that it doesn't get forgotten in the midst of the busyness of life.

Oral Health

If you don't have dental insurance, you may be able to reduce the cost of routine checks and more intensive dental care by paying cash or scheduling multiple appointments at the same time. Our motto is it never hurts to ask!

Although it may seem counterintuitive, regular dental care saves you money in the long term by keeping your teeth and gums healthier and catching any problems earlier. Most experts recommend visiting the dentist every six to twelve months.

As with most health-care appointments, the "best" time to schedule regular checkups is first thing in the morning, before the office gets backed up with other patients and emergencies. When possible, schedule multiple family members at once to reduce waiting and travel time.

Most of us have been in a situation where we didn't have a

Tips for Whiter Teeth

These days, over-the-counter teeth whitening kits are hugely popular. We all want bright white smiles, right? Besides the cost of the kits, there's also some concern that overdoing it can cause increased sensitivity in the teeth and enamel damage (kits should be used no more than twice a year). However, you can achieve the same effects at home by brushing with a baking-soda-and-hydrogen-peroxide mix.

To keep teeth at their whitest, brush immediately after eating the dark foods and drinks listed below:

- dark chocolate
- tea
- coffee
- soda
- blueberries
- red wine

toothbrush and needed one, whether after a sugary dessert or while away from home for the day. Eating an apple, rinsing your mouth with hot water for thirty seconds, or chewing certain gums make your teeth feel cleaner when you can't brush, but they're definitely not replacements for regular brushing. Keep in mind that you should replace your toothbrush every three to four months to make sure that it's effective and not harboring bacteria.

Prescriptions

Drugstore pharmacies often offer prescription coupons to entice new customers. It's tempting to switch your prescription medicines from pharmacy to pharmacy to take advantage of these coupons, but professionals discourage this practice because it increases the risk of error. Having multiple prescriptions at different pharmacies substantially increases your risk of inadvertently taking medications that don't interact well. Instead, ask your current pharmacy if they're willing to accept competitor coupons so that you can keep your prescriptions in one place and still take advantage of available discounts.

Ask your doctor about the generic formulation of any medications you need. Many insurance providers discount your copay on generics, and if you're paying out of pocket, you'll save a significant amount of money on generics. Likewise, ask your doctor about splitting your pills. You can often purchase a thirty-day supply of medicine with a larger dosage for the same cost as the lesser dose. If you split the higher dosage pills in half, they'll last twice as long. You'll need to discuss this option with your doctor since not all pills can be split in half and only he or she can write you a prescription for the larger dosage, but if your doctor agrees, purchase an inexpensive pill splitter from your pharmacy to split the pills rather than trying to do it with a knife.

Although they often promise lower prices, be wary of online pharmacies, many of which aren't accredited and sell expired and counterfeit drugs. There *are* legitimate online pharmacies, but it's best to stick with VIPPS-accredited pharmacies (http:// allingoodtime.net/VIPPS) that have been vetted by the National Association of Boards of Pharmacy.

Walmart and Target both offer a variety of common prescription drugs for just $4, so be sure to check your prescription against their list, especially if your insurance doesn't cover prescription medicine or you need to get regular refills. Many grocery stores also offer free antibiotics (http://allingoodtime.net/prescriptions).

If possible, the best time to fill a prescription is during the day, when a lot of people are still at work. If you're not able to get to the pharmacy, ask your doctor's office if they'd be willing to fax the prescription so that it will be ready when you go to pick it up.

TIP: Remembering to take vitamins or prescriptions can be a hassle, and the best way to make sure you take them when you're supposed to is to associate them with a regular routine. For example, many people take their daily vitamins every day with breakfast. For medicines that should be taken on an empty stomach, keep them in your bathroom and take them first thing in the morning before you start getting ready for the day. For children who need medicine regularly, the same holds true—giving medicine at the same time of day as part of a routine is a great way to make sure it doesn't get forgotten.

For someone who needs multiple medicines several times a day, a pill dispenser or organizer is a valuable tool to help you keep track of what has or has not been taken. Don't leave important things like this to chance since it can be hard to remember whether you've taken your pills today . . . or was that yesterday?

Skin Screenings

Like regular breast cancer screenings, yearly skin screenings are also an important part of preventive health care, especially for individuals who have lots of moles or freckles. To make sure you don't forget your yearly exam, make your appointment for next year while you're checking out at the doctor's office. If you've made a yearly appointment with yourself to review insurance, wills and other financial and legal documents, use that time to schedule yearly exams and appointments as well.

Surgical Procedures

If your insurance coverage does not fully cover medical expenses or procedures, *always* ask your health-care provider what discounts they're willing to offer. Many will offer a cash discount if you're willing to pay in full, and you may qualify for additional discounts as well.

When you need emergency surgery, the last thing on your mind is the "best" time to have it done, but if you're having an elective or nonemergency surgery done, try to avoid holidays, when hospitals may have less staff on hand. In general, scheduling surgeries in the morning reduces the likelihood of having your appointment bumped because of emergencies. It's also been documented that more medical mistakes are made during shift changes than at any other time, so if you can avoid scheduling a surgery or hospital stay near a shift change, you probably should.

SALON/SPA TREATMENTS

With the advent of group buying sites, like Groupon and Living Social (http://allingoodtime.net/dailydeals), finding bargains on salon treatments may only be a mouse click away. Register to receive alerts for your location and let the deals come to you! We've seen salon treatments priced at 50 percent off and lower recently.

Each year, Spa Week hosts two weeklong events where participating spas offer their very best treatments for just $50! (http://allingoodtime.net/spaweek)

SHOWER

We don't know about you, but when it comes to deciding between saving money with shorter showers or enjoying the brief respite from "real" life, we usually opt for the latter. Both of us have been known to do our best thinking in the shower, and a shower is a great way to get your focus at the beginning of the day or relax and recharge after a busy day!

If you're committed to conserving water in order to live green or to reduce your water bill, though, use a bucket to catch the wasted water that runs while you wait for it to heat up. Use this for watering plants inside or out or even for filling a water table for your kids. You'll also want to be sure to use a water-efficient showerhead to avoid wasted water.

To reduce the time you spend in the shower, consider using an electric shaver for your legs or turning off the water while you scrub your hair. If you need some extra motivation, set a timer and see if you can beat your best time . . . without sacrificing cleanliness, of course.

If you have trouble fitting a shower into a busy day (and let's face it, most busy parents have dealt with that at one time or another), try setting your alarm just fifteen minutes earlier and hopping in before the kids are up for the day. If you have older kids, have them start their breakfast or morning routine while you're in the shower. Alternatively, we often take showers at night so that we can take our time without feeling as rushed.

If you have younger kids who are always up before you, create a basket of activities to keep them busy in the bathroom or a nearby room (Pack 'n Plays and play yards are great for busy toddlers), and be sure to teach them the rules about answering the phone or door while you're in the shower.

Because shower time is often free from distractions, we tend to have our best ideas while in there. Keep a glass memo board and dry-erase marker or bath crayons in the shower so that you can write down your ideas, to-do lists, and other reminders as you think of them!

Use Every Last Bit

Saving money often means using what you have rather than running out to buy replacements, and the same can be said for the last bits of toothpaste, shampoo, and gel in the containers. It's tempting to simply toss the bottles or tubes rather than deal with the frustration of trying to squeeze the last little bit out, so Mandi usually keeps hers hidden away until there's really none left. Here are some tips for getting the last bits out of various containers.

TOOTHPASTE TUBE:

While you can purchase commercial products that keep your toothpaste tube rolled from the end as you go, you can also use a chip clip or paper clip to do the same thing. Or, just squeeze from the bottom each time, and you don't even need to keep it rolled to get all of the toothpaste out!

HAIR GEL, FACE WASH, AND OTHER STANDING TUBES:

The shape and thickness of these larger "standing" tubes makes them much harder to straighten and squeeze. Amanda from OhAmanda.com shared this tip to get the last bits out. Once you've squeezed as much as you can out of the tube, cut it in half (from side to side) with sharp scissors. You'll be able to scoop out what's left in both halves, and chances are you'll find at least two to three days' worth of product left in there!

SHAMPOO AND CONDITIONER:

We keep our bottles turned upside down to make it easier to squeeze those last bits out, but sometimes that's just not enough. When no more will come out, add some water to the bottle, swish it around, and then pour it directly onto your head. You should cut enough suds for one more good wash.

Bedroom

BEDDING

As with towel linens, January is the best time of year to purchase bedding at low, low prices. You'll find great prices at Kohl's, Target, and other superstores, but if you're looking for high-quality brand names, shop during the department-store white sales. Take advantage of department-store coupons for even deeper discounts! You can also find great deals on brand-name bedding all year round at discount stores like T.J.Maxx and HomeGoods, but your selection will be more limited than during the white sales.

Rather than worrying about thread count, pay attention to the type of thread used in your sheets. One hundred percent cotton sheets are softer and cooler than cotton-polyester blends. Egyptian and Supima cotton makes sheets noticeably softer, as does bamboo, and according to RealSimple.com, you're better off investing in a lower thread count made from these fibers than a higher thread count made from cotton-polyester blend.

Sheets should be changed every one to two weeks because of the amount of skin cells that we shed each day. Although it's a good idea to keep a spare set of sheets on hand for emergencies and accidents, Mandi typically washes and dries her sheets and puts them straight back on the bed to avoid having to fold them. Blankets and comforters that are used over sheets should be washed once every one to two months. Be sure to keep this in mind when choosing a comforter because getting your comforter dry-cleaned that often isn't exactly cheap or convenient!

TIP: In the midst of busy family life, a week or two can pass in the blink of an eye. To avoid the "when was the last time we washed the sheets?" syndrome, schedule your sheet washing with other routine events or chores. Wash the master bedroom sheets each Tuesday or on each payday. Have kids bring their sheets to the laundry room every Saturday morning before turning on the cartoons. Creating routines that you can do automatically without having to stop to think is a great way to save time and mental energy.

QUICK TIP: Fitted sheets can be a pain to fold and often take up extra space in the linen closet. Watch Mandi's trick for folding fitted sheets and towels at http://allingoodtime.net/linens.

Creating a Haven in Your Master Bedroom

Your master bedroom should be a haven from the stresses of life, not just because it's nice to have a place to call your own but also because it will actually help you to sleep better! Creating a haven doesn't have to involve a lot of time or money. Here are a few simple ways to get started today:

- Don't use your bedroom as a storage room. We know it's tempting to stick things in your room when they don't have a home, but resist the urge and try to keep your bedroom clutter-free!
- Choose colors that reflect the mood you want for your room. Decorate with neutral colors for a serene retreat, dark and rich colors for a luxurious space, or splashes of bright color for a refreshing and invigorating tone.
- Minimize knickknacks. Rather than covering the surfaces with knickknacks and mementos, choose a few that you really love.
- Make space to sit and relax as well as sleep. Depending on the size of your room, you may want to add a seating area or simply buy some big pillows that you can sit up against on the bed. Having a place to sit is a great way to hide away and recharge even for just five minutes at a time.

CLOTHING

For the best deals on clothing, shop midseason when retailers start putting seasonal items on clearance to make room for the next season (is it just us, or is this happening earlier and earlier every year?). You'll find great deals on staples such as jeans from October through December as retailers try to entice shoppers into their stores.

Thrifting is a great way to expand your wardrobe without spending a ton of money, especially if you shop the thrift stores in more affluent areas. The trade-off, though, is that you have to be willing to invest the time to shop regularly and dig through the clothing to find really great pieces. Tara has always enjoyed hunting for deals, but Mandi would rather spend more to save time. Only you can decide whether saving time or saving money is more important to you at your current stage of life, and it will probably vary throughout different stages!

When thrift-shopping, always try things on before you purchase them so that you don't end up with more things than you don't really care for. Find out your stores' regular sale days, when items are marked down even lower, and always carry cash when visiting a new store in case they don't accept credit or debit cards. Most importantly, be willing to say no to a great deal if you don't love it or aren't sure you'll wear it, since a couple dollars here and a couple dollars there can add up over time if you're not careful.

TIP: Before you shop, clean out the clothes currently in your closet. You'll have an easier time making a decision on what to wear when you truly love the clothes in your closet and aren't distracted by the clothes that you don't really like and hardly wear. Like most areas of our lives and homes, we can apply the 80/20 rule here. Most people wear 20 percent of their clothes 80 percent the time. Decluttering your closet to get rid of the clothing that you don't wear makes it easier to find the things you love and put away clean laundry and reduces the time and energy you spend thinking about what to wear.

One great way to see what you do or don't wear is to hang all of your hangers backward at the beginning of the season. As you remove items to wear them, hang the hanger at the front of the closet and then, when you're putting your laundry away, hang them correctly. It won't take very long to see which clothes you actually wear.

Coats

When shopping for new coats, you'll find the best combination of price and selection in December, as retailers offer holiday sales while they still have generous stocks. Prices will dip lower in January, but you may be disappointed with the remaining sizes and styles.

Storage

In most areas, winter coats need to be stored for at least half of the year. Properly storing coats keeps them from being damaged while in storage so that they last longer and can be used year after year or passed on to someone else.

Before storing coats, wash them or have them dry-cleaned. If you store your coats in a closet, use cedar hangers to deter insects, or if storage space is limited, pack them in under-the-bed boxes. Avoid storing coats in moist areas where they may get mildewed, and pack them in breathable covered boxes or use garment bags to keep them from collecting dust.

TIP: To save time next winter, repair coats and jackets before packing them away so that they'll be ready for use when needed!

Hosiery/Lingerie

Although there are plenty of things that you can buy used to save money, undergarments, hosiery, and lingerie aren't among them. Neither of us wears panty hose regularly, but Tara prefers the department-store brands because they feel nicer and last longer, while Mandi prefers the least expensive brands because she always seems to cause runs in them (regardless of the quality) and she doesn't feel as bad when she's only spent three dollars on a pair.

Lingerie goes on sale pretty regularly, and knowing the sales cycles of your favorite store is the best way to get great deals. For example, Victoria's Secret hosts a semiannual sale every January and June, and you'll find big bargains then. You'll also find deals on lingerie after Valentine's Day and during the early summer when stores are trying to appeal to new brides.

Caring for Lingerie

To keep lingerie and hosiery from getting snagged or torn in the wash, use a mesh lingerie bag, which keeps it separate from the rest of the load and protects it from zippers and Velcro. You can often find these in the dollar section at stores, so keep several on hand. To prevent pilling, turn your hosiery inside out before putting it in the wash.

Also check the tags on lingerie before tossing in the dryer

because one of us (we're not telling who!) has ruined some of her favorites by doing just that! The elastic and padding in bras can quickly lose its shape if it's sent through the dryer each time they're washed. Instead, pull these items out and let them air-dry. And note that most hosiery and lingerie shouldn't be hung to dry but should be laid flat on a breathable surface so that it doesn't get misshapen.

Pajamas

Pajamas are a popular Christmas gift, so you're likely to find lots of sales and specials during November. However, pajamas also make great gifts year-round, so consider stocking up for various birthdays during these sales.

We both have a tradition of getting our children new pajamas for Christmas. They all look forward to opening them on Christmas Eve every year, and as an added bonus, they make for extra-cute photos on Christmas morning.

JEWELRY

When it comes to jewelry purchases, it pays to focus more on when not to buy—Christmas, Valentine's Day, and Mother's Day. Jewelers will be more open to negotiating when they don't have the high traffic these holidays generally bring.

TIP: Although both of us do a lot of our shopping online, we're leery of buying fine jewelry online since you can't really see the quality or try it on before purchasing. Tara and her husband have been going to the same jeweler since before they were married, and there's something to be said for building lasting relationships for higher-end purchases, since a jeweler is more likely to give a repeat customer a discount. The prices in jewelry stores are *always* negotiable, and you shouldn't pay more than 60 to 70 percent of the sticker price. To get the best price possible, start by offering them 50 percent of the list price and negotiate from there. Offer cash, if possible, which saves the jeweler the 3 percent credit-card processing fees and may help you negotiate for a better price.

For everyday jewelry, we both love the hand-stamped and unique (dare we say funky?) pieces you can find at Etsy.com. You'll find something for virtually every budget, from stamped jewelry celebrating the people you love to jewelry made from repurposed materials such as reclaimed glass, book pages, old maps, and other vintage items.

Maintenance

Many times, you can take your jewelry back to your jeweler to be cleaned on the spot. Mandi regularly cleans her engagement ring with a baking-soda toothpaste and a toothbrush (specially designated for cleaning her ring) at home, although many jewelers recommend against this method because it can scratch certain soft stones (such as amber, lapis, turquoise) and damage metals. As with anything, the key is moderation.

MATTRESSES

Since your mattress plays such a huge role in whether you get a good night's sleep, it's better to focus more on your needs than on getting the lowest price. Find the mattress that best fits your needs, and then watch for a good sale on it. Mattresses typically go on sale for 50 percent off, though, so don't pay retail! Be sure to haggle, especially at independent retailers, to get the best price possible.

That doesn't mean that you need to spend a ton of money on a top-of-the-line mattress, though. Mandi and her husband have been using an IKEA foam mattress that they bought for less than $200 for almost five years now, and they're still very happy with it!

According to Martha Stewart, non-pillowtop mattresses should be flipped and all mattresses rotated four times a year. They should be flipped over as well as rotated from head to toe to ensure that they don't become unevenly warn. She suggests pinning a card to each end labeled with January (right side up) and April (upside down) on one card and July (right side up) and October (upside down) on the other. Turn the mattress each quarter so that the correct month is facing up at the foot of the bed to make sure that you're evenly rotating it. Even with good care, mattresses need to be replaced at least every ten years or when you find yourself waking up feeling stiff and sore.

TIP: Although you may have jokingly told your children, "Sleep tight. Don't let the bedbugs bite!" bedbugs are actually an increasing problem in many areas of the United States. These insects are about the size of an apple seed and, like mosquitoes, survive on human blood. Although they're big enough to see, they're nocturnal, so you can have an infestation and not know it until you develop a skin rash or allergic symptoms.

Preventing Bedbugs

So, how do you prevent bedbugs? Because the bugs are transported on luggage, mattresses, and furniture, it's important to carefully check any secondhand furniture you buy, as well as your luggage after traveling.

Eliminating bedbugs once there is an infestation is difficult, time-consuming, and costly, so it's worth being extra careful beforehand. Mattress protectors not only help eliminate allergens but also keep bedbugs from moving in, and they may be a wise investment!

If you do suspect a bedbug infestation, it's best to hire a professional immediately. There are nonchemical ways to get rid of them—including placing clothing, furniture, and other items in either extreme heat (such as the dryer or in plastic wrapping outside in the summer) or extreme cold (such as a chest freezer or outside in the winter)—but mattresses and box springs often have to be thrown away, and extermination only works if you kill all of the bedbugs.

PILLOWS

Pillows are on sale frequently year-round. Watch for buy-one-get-one-free sales in particular to get the most for your money. According to WebMD, you should choose a pillow based on your sleep style. If you sleep on your back, use a thin pillow. Shaped pillows that cradle your neck are even better. Similarly, stomach sleepers should use very thin, almost flat pillows. Side

Hosting Overnight Guests

Preparing for overnight guests can be stressful, but it doesn't have to be! While there may be a few picky people like your aunt Stella who notice every dust bunny and point out every fault, most guests are understanding and happy to just spend time with you and your family (that's why they're there, after all, isn't it?). Here are a few ways you can pamper your guests during their stay:

- Make sure you have enough bed linens, pillows, and blankets.
- Lay out towels and washcloths where they're easy to find.
- Buy snacks and drinks that your guests like.
- Put a basket of snacks in their room in case they're hungry and don't want to disturb you.
- Keep extra toiletries on hand in case they forget anything.
- Store extra toilet paper in the guest room so they can get a new roll as needed.
- Clear space for their suitcase and clothes so they can unpack, if possible.
- Find out about any sleeping preferences, such as a TV, fan, or other white noise.

sleepers, on the other hand, need thick firm pillows to properly support their head and neck.

Use pillow protectors underneath your sheets and pillowcases as an extra layer of protection. While pillows can be washed in the washing machine, cheap ones will often lose their shape and firmness, and the less you have to wash any pillow, the longer it will last.

When you do wash them, try running two together to help your machines stay balanced and give them an extra rinse to be sure you get all residue out. Dry on the air cycle or low heat to prevent clumping, but always be sure they're fully dry to prevent mold growth.

PURSES

We have different philosophies when it comes to purses. Mandi only started carrying one recently (now that her kids have outgrown the need for diaper bags), and she usually sticks with her SnapTotes photo purse or a hobo bag she picked up on clearance at Target. Tara, who's the more fashionable one between us, enjoys name-brand purses—although she still always looks for great deals on them!

Tara prefers to purchase purses online to get the lowest prices. Be sure to stick to reputable sites (http://allingoodtime .net/purses) to ensure that you're getting the real thing when it comes to designer goods. If you're unsure whether an item you find in a thrift shop or garage sale is the real thing or an illegal knockoff, check the stitching, details, labels, and—if possible— the original packaging. If you're buying from a discount store and the deal seems too good to be true, it probably is!

TIP: If you are a purse collector, consider a purse organizer such as the Pouchee or Kangaroo Keeper, which allows you to quickly move your things between purses.

Storage

To store your purses so that they don't get damaged or forgotten, try a hanging sweater organizer (yes, we love those things!) or open baskets or shelving. Hanging purses from hangers or hooks can damage the straps, and storing them inside tightly closed containers can lead to moisture damage. For purses that will be stored long term, you may want to stuff them to help them keep their shape and use a fabric storage bag to keep them from getting dusty.

SHOES

Our friend Shannon Shaffer, who blogs at FortheMommas.com and is a self-proclaimed frugalista, also happens to love good-quality shoes. Since you'll find us in flip-flops as often as we can get away with it, we asked Shannon for her best shoe-shopping tips.

Buying inexpensive shoes can save you money up front, but Shannon points out that it often costs more over time. Quality shoes can literally last years, even with daily wear, because they're usually real leather rather than man-made materials. They also fit better and more comfortably, so you're less likely to have sore feet at the end of the day. This doesn't mean that all expensive shoes are good quality, though. In many cases, you're paying more money for a designer label rather than a quality shoe. The best thing you can do is actually try shoes on in the store to find a pair that fits comfortably. Once you are familiar with a brand, you can buy online, but you may not want to spend a lot of money on a shoe that you've never tried on before. Zappos is the exception to this rule because of their generous 365-day return policy, which means you won't be stuck with an uncomfortable pair of shoes.

Buy quality shoes for less by shopping off-season. That means picking up boots in the spring and sandals in the fall even though you won't get to wear them until next year. If you buy classic styles rather than the latest trends, you won't have to worry about them going out of style in the meantime. Zappos and eBay also offer deep discounts on shoes; just make sure you're looking at new shoes on eBay. Department stores often release percentage-off coupons that you can use to pick up a great pair of shoes as well.

Storage

To help shoes last longer, store them on shelves or racks rather than in piles so that they don't get misshapen or scratched. For high-quality shoes, you may want to invest in cedar shoe trees that can be inserted into the shoe to help it keep its shape. These also reduce moisture and absorb odor to keep your shoes fresh.

It's important to keep shoes clean and dry. In the winter, place damp shoes near a heating vent to help them dry more quickly.

TIP: There are plenty of commercial products for smelly shoes, but you can also try washing shoes—either in the washing machine or by hand—and/or sprinkling them with baking soda, which you simply shake out when you're ready to wear them.

SLEEPING/WAKING UP

Most of us don't need to be reminded of the importance of a good night's sleep, but sometimes that's easier said than done. Nursing babies, sick kids, special projects, and busy days all keep us from getting the sleep we need—along with Facebook, blogs, books, and the TV!

According to the National Sleep Foundation, we all have different sleep needs, but most adults need seven to nine hours of sleep a night. Getting less sleep on a regular basis can lead to a sleep debt that causes obesity, high blood pressure, irritability, decreased productivity, and safety issues.

That's all well and good to know in theory, but how do we actually make sure we get enough sleep? Sometimes we just need to decide that we will go to bed at a certain time each night, regardless of how riveting that made-for-TV movie is or what's happening on Facebook. If you're staying up to work on a big project, it's important to remember that your productivity actually goes down when you're sleep deprived, and a good night's sleep may actually help you get more done the next day.

If you have trouble falling asleep, a good bedtime routine may help. Many experts recommend turning off all electronics—including the TV—at least an hour before you go to bed. As part of your bedtime routine, you might also wash your face with a warm washcloth, change into cozy pajamas, and relax with a good book.

Sometimes, even when we are getting adequate sleep, it can be hard to get out of bed in the morning. While Tara is a night owl, Mandi is an early bird and prefers the early morning hours to get a head start on the day. During the winter, this means waking up to a cold, dark house, so she keeps a warm sweater and slippers by her bed. On days when she's feeling sluggish and needs to get moving, she splashes cold water on her face and drinks a full glass of water as well. A few jumping jacks or stretches can also get your blood pumping, even without the help of caffeine.

TIP: Water with lemon isn't just a taste preference. Lemon water actually helps improve your circulation, and drinking a glass in the morning is a great way to start your day (http://allingoodtime.net/lemonwater)!

An important part of feeling rested is going to bed and waking up at the same time each day. Of course there will be exceptions, but in general, doing so gives your body a natural rhythm so that it's easier to fall asleep and wake up each day.

SUNGLASSES

According to Lifehacker, most brand-name sunglasses are actually manufactured by the same Italian company, Luxottica. The difference in price comes purely from the branding. Experts suggest that you can get a quality pair of sunglasses with the same UV protection as high-end branded sunglasses for just about $40. To save even more, forgo the polarized lenses unless you plan to spend a significant time around water.

Tips for Falling Asleep

There is nothing worse than being tired and wanting to sleep but not being able to fall asleep. Try these tricks to get the sleep you want (although we recommend making an appointment with your doctor if you have chronic insomnia!):

- Count backward from one hundred.
- Close your eyes but try to stay awake.
- Take a shower.
- Drink a warm cup of milk or chamomile tea.
- Think through happy memories and special moments.
- Relax and try not to stress about missed sleep, which just makes it harder to fall asleep.
- Place a lavender sachet under your pillow to help you fall asleep and sleep better.
- Ask your doctor about natural sleep aids such as melatonin and valerian.

SWIMWEAR

Swimwear starts appearing in stores as early as February these days, with sales starting in the early summer. Although the lowest prices appear in August and September, you'll have less selection to choose from.

If you're looking for a swimsuit that you can wear year after year, invest in a quality suit from Victoria's Secret or Lands' End. If you prefer trendier suits that you can update each year without feeling guilty, Target, Kohl's, and Old Navy all offer a wide selection at great prices.

Swimwear should be washed every time you wear it, but washing machines can quickly shorten the life of your suit. Hand-wash your bathing suit as soon as you take it off to extend its life, and—like lingerie—avoid putting swimsuits in the dryer since the heat can ruin the elasticity.

Dining Room/ Living Room

CHINA/DRINKWARE/ SERVEWARE

The best time to buy china is in June, which is also the most popular month for weddings, since stores are discounting place settings to encourage guests to purchase them as gifts. For a more creative approach, purchase mismatched pieces from thrift stores over time, which can make for a beautiful table with a variety of patterns artfully mixed together.

TIP: Although we don't have china sets ourselves—for our families, they're simply another expense and another item that sits in storage and doesn't get used—we know that many families do keep a set for entertaining and special occasions. If you have a set of china that doesn't get used enough, either consider selling it or giving it away. If you use it occasionally, consider pulling it out more often—maybe as a Sunday-night dinner tradition or for birthdays and anniversaries rather than just holidays and entertaining.

Storage

According to "Hints from Heloise," the best way to store China is with tissue paper, coffee filters, or paper plates between them to prevent scratching. Be careful not to stack them too high, especially old or delicate china, because the weight could crack or damage the pieces at the bottom of the stacks. Always store china in an area with moderate temperatures, as extreme temperatures can also cause cracking.

Maintenance

To keep china looking beautiful for years to come, rinse pieces as soon as you're done eating to prevent stains, and never use silverware to scrape leftover food from the plate, since it can scratch or mar the surface. Use a mild soap and warm (but not hot) water to wash the dishes and dry them by hand to prevent water spots. See the sidebar for more tips on restoring china that has become damaged or stained.

Restoring Damaged China

To remove stains:

1. Sprinkle a soft cloth with baking soda or salt.
2. Sprinkle a damp sponge with cream of tartar.
3. For hard-water stains, fill a tub with warm water and add

a few citrus rinds and then soak dishes overnight in the mixture.

4. Add a little toothpaste to a soft cloth and gently rub silverware marks.

5. To repair spidery surface cracks, place the china in a pan of warm milk for thirty minutes.

Most importantly, just relax and enjoy your time with friends and family rather than worrying about having everything perfect or meeting other people's expectations!

(FROM DOITYOURSELF.COM)

DECOR

The best time to purchase table decor, including centerpieces, place-card holders, and napkin rings, is after the major holidays. Look for neutral colors that can actually be used year-round. We also recommend shopping at the major crafts store. It takes some patience, but they regularly issue coupons for 40 percent off one item in the store, and you could pick up any larger pieces you need at a great price using these.

FRAMES

There tend to be a lot of sales on picture frames before the "Hallmark Holidays" like Mother's Day, Father's Day, etc. However, you also might consider the craft stores to pick up unfinished frames that you can customize. Digital frames are coming down in price and make a really nice gift, especially the new Wi-Fi-enabled frames that allow you to email new photos directly to them, perfect for family members that aren't very tech savvy.

LAMPS

There isn't really a best time of year to buy lamps, but you can often find fantastic prices on high-end lamps at off-price stores like T.J.Maxx and Marshalls. Tara found a beautiful set of matched lamps with the shades intact for $19.95 each, and we have no doubt that a single lamp would have retailed for much more than she paid for the pair.

For other decor, such as prints, vases, or candles, be sure to watch the clearance sales at Target, Crate & Barrel, and other similar stores. They frequently rotate their stock, discounting the older styles for up to 75 percent off, but you'll have to check back regularly to find the pieces you want at the best price!

If you don't have the patience for clearance sales, then stores like IKEA, T.J.Maxx, HomeGoods, and Tuesday Morning offer great deals on decor all year round.

FLOORING

Rather than telling you the best time to buy flooring, let's start with when is NOT a good time to buy flooring. Many people use their tax returns to make home renovations, so late February through the end of April is a busy time in the flooring industry. July and August are also busier months because a lot of people are remodeling before the school year begins. And mid-October through mid-December is busy as people are looking to spruce up their homes for holiday gatherings. Your chances of getting a discount are far greater outside of these high traffic periods, but regardless of the time of year you're buying, don't expect to get the lowest prices at a chain store, such as Home Depot or Lowe's. Locally owned carpet dealers and flooring retailers typically have more leeway on pricing, so head to your local stores in late December or early January for the best deals possible.

TIP: Carpet can quickly get dirty and worn out in the high traffic areas of a busy household. Cut down on the wear and tear with a shoes-off policy in the house. To make this easier, keep a bench or chair near your entryway as well as a rack or bin for shoes. Vacuuming often, even when your carpet doesn't look dirty, actually extends the life of your carpet by removing dirt that may be wearing down the carpet as you walk over the surface.

Hardwood Flooring

Wood is the biggest expense in hardwood flooring, so consider using laminate instead for the same look at a fraction of the cost. If your heart truly desires real hardwood floors, consider installing it yourself to save on installation.

Mandi's husband actually custom-made their hardwood floor by hand out of sheets of birch plywood that he cut, stained, and sealed. It was very time intensive, but it definitely saved them money in the process!

Maintenance

We've both found that with kids and dogs in the house, it's worth investing in a good steam cleaner, for spills of all sizes as well as regular deep cleaning. Steam cleaners with attachments also make it easy to steam-clean couches and other upholstery.

When Mandi and her husband built their new home, they opted for wood floors instead of carpet to eliminate potential allergens and the additional maintenance of carpet. There is a trade-off, as wood and tile floors tend to be colder, but a few rugs can warm up the areas you use most often.

FRESH FLOWERS

While fresh flowers are definitely a splurge and not a necessity, we both love to brighten up our homes with a vase full of fresh cut flowers. Whether you're buying flowers for yourself or for someone special in your life, try to avoid the big holidays like Mother's Day and Valentine's Day, when florists mark prices up. Whenever you buy, think outside of the traditional florists. Grocers and discount stores like Trader Joe's and ALDI offer beautiful bouquets for a steal, and Costco has professional-quality flowers.

When buying arrangements online as gifts, be sure to search for promo codes before submitting your order. There's almost always one available for each of the major companies.

If you have a green thumb, a flowering plant is a less expensive and healthier alternative. Tara keeps several in her office, but Mandi has killed too many to count.

TIP: Our favorite flowers include tulips and lilies, but we also like inexpensive bouquets of carnations and daisies because they last for so long. Whatever type of flowers you prefer, keep them around longer by removing any leaves that sit below the waterline and cutting the bottom of the stems at an angle under running water. We've heard people say that adding a tarnished penny to the bottom of the vase will make flowers last longer, so we tested this side by side with a vase with a teaspoon of bleach and a vase with the flower food that comes with cut flowers. The flowers in the vase with the flower food outlasted both of the frugal alternatives, with the bleach water coming in a close second. Unfortunately, the flowers in the vase with the tarnished penny wilted before the rest.

FURNITURE

February is the best time to buy new furniture because the heavy entertaining season is over and new models are making their way to showroom floors, so retailers will be looking to rid themselves of older stock to make way for these new models.

Entertaining When You're Short on Time and Money

Shaina from FoodforMyFamily.com offers these tips for entertaining when you're on a budget or short on time.

ATMOSPHERE:
- Put flowers from your garden in a simple vase or even a glass jar.
- Although it means more cleanup, opt for real dinnerware rather than paper and plastic.
- Use a tablecloth to add specialness to the occasion and hide imperfections in your table, and set the table before your guests arrive.
- Even if you're only serving tea, punch, or lemonade, use wineglasses for dinner.
- Serve small desserts like cookies, brownies, and tarts on a tiered cake stand to create a big statement without any extra work.
- During the warmer months, have a lawn party with picnic blankets or tables to avoid having to clean your whole house!
- Plan a few fun party games that make the party more about the people and less about the place or food.

FOOD:
- If you're looking for inexpensive and easy food, try tacos or fajitas or grill marinated chicken skewers.
- Serve vegetables with a variety of dips for a fun and easy appetizer.

- Fill phyllo shells with a sweet or savory filling for a special touch that doesn't take too much time.
- Drizzle oil over homemade hummus and serve with pitas and vegetables.

Find out if your favorite retailer has a seconds store in your area or ask if they're offering any discounts on their floor samples. Tara and her husband purchased a leather couch that retailed for $2,000 on the showroom floor for just over $300 at the local seconds showroom because of a tiny scuff on the arm that was barely noticeable. Remember that new items only look "new" for so long anyhow.

Much of the furniture in Mandi's home is from IKEA, which offers modern decor that fits almost any budget. These huge stores have tons of selection to choose from, although you have to be willing to transport and assemble your pieces.

If you are patient and live near a larger city, you can often buy used high-end furniture in good condition at a deep discount on Craigslist or at an estate sale.

Finally, thrifting is a great way to find furniture for your home that matches your style without breaking the bank. Myra from CasabellaProject.com is a thrift-shopping queen, and she shared these tips with us:

- Although you shouldn't buy anything and everything you see when thrift-shopping, it's important not to go with too many expectations. You won't always find what you're looking for on the first, second, or third trip out, but if you keep your eyes open, you're likely to find other treasures that you can use in ways that you might not have thought of outside of the thrift store. Prices vary between thrift shops, but you'll be able to spot which are overpriced over time. Myra says she never pays more than $5 for an individual piece of home decor and no more than $40 for a piece of furniture.

- It might feel overwhelming to consider refinishing or repurposing furniture if you don't have any experience, but most home decor can be given "new life" with a simple coat of spray paint. The most important thing to remember is that thrift-store stock changes frequently, so check back often for the best variety and deals.

HOSTESS GIFTS

If you're a busy mom, running out to buy a hostess gift isn't always convenient, especially at the end of a long week. Instead, keep a gift closet stocked with gifts so that you can choose something that reflects the personality and style of your hostess. It doesn't hurt that you can usually purchase gifts for less this way because you can stock up during seasonal sales and clearances!

Stock up on discounted gift baskets after Christmas or piece together items as you come across them. We both love Lands' End's colorful canvas totes, which you can find at 50 percent off throughout the year. Fill one with a few themed items, and you've got a fantastic gift that any hostess will appreciate.

More Hostess Gift Ideas

For a casual barbecue or lunch date: a set of nice reusable shopping bags

For the foodie: a potted herb or special olive oil

For the life of the party : a party game or set of conversation starters

For the traditional one: a set of pretty stationery

For your boss: a nice pen set

For a young family: a movie-night basket or family board game

For neighbors: a potted flower or hanging flower basket

For your best friend: a spa certificate and offer to babysit

For someone you don't know well: a pretty scented candle or a picture frame

For the coffee lover: a nice travel mug and gift card to Starbucks or favorite coffee spot

For the intellectual: a puzzle or a gift card to their local bookstore

SILVERWARE

Most people buy new flatware when they're planning to entertain, but you won't find much of a price break in November and December. However, stores are eager to get rid of overstock after the holidays, so look for sales then. You also may find savings in March as retailers look to sell out last year's patterns as well as in September when the wedding season is winding down.

Like china, both of us tend to stick to our everyday flatware set rather than keeping a special set of actual *silver*ware. However, if you have a special set of actual *silver*ware, chances are you've dealt with tarnished silver a time or two already. For less expensive and quicker cleaning, try soaking your silver in a bowl of vinegar for twenty-four hours. Then rub it gently with a soft brush and rinse well with warm water to remove any residue. Although the total cleaning time is longer than other methods, it's less time intensive than rubbing each spot away by hand!

TABLE LINENS/CLOTH NAPKINS

Table linens and cloth napkins are a fantastic way to add a little personality to a table setting, and they shouldn't be reserved just for special occasions. Cloth napkins are actually very environmentally friendly, saving you a bundle on purchasing paper towels and paper napkins. Thrift stores are a fabulous resource for inexpensive table linens and cloth napkins, and Mandi's family actually purchased their inexpensive cloth napkins new at IKEA. Be sure to keep an eye on the clearance aisles after holidays because you can often find deep discounts on holiday merchandise that can be used all year long.

VACUUMS

New vacuum-cleaner models arrive in stores in June, making April and May prime time for discounts. Tara is partial to Dyson brand vacuums. Not only are they aesthetically pleasing, but they also have a pretty compelling breakdown on their site comparing the costs of ownership over a five-year period since there are no bags, belts, or filters to buy (http://allingood time.net/dyson). Mandi's family has both an Electrolux Versatility and an Ergorapido Stick and hand vac, both of which they love. We both have tried the robotic vacuums without much success, and we recommend using a small stick vac for quick cleanup around the kitchen and high traffic areas since you're more likely to actually do it if it's convenient and easy. Then you can reserve your regular upright for more in-depth cleaning.

To keep your vacuum performing at its best, be sure to clean the brush and roller regularly. In Mandi's home—with a mom and four little girls with long hair—this is almost a weekly task!

Home Office

BANKING

Choosing a Bank

When choosing a new bank, it's important to look at account fees and get feedback from other customers. Most banks offer free checking and savings accounts these days, but they may have different required minimum balances, overdraft fees, and online banking systems. The best bank is one that offers convenience and affordability, so we recommend looking for a bank that offers overdraft protection (usually this works by pulling money from a designated savings account if needed) and allows you to pay bills and access old checks and statements online.

If you don't have a lot of cash to deposit, you may find that an Internet bank like ING Direct (http://allingoodtime.net/

ingdirect) is a better solution since you save money on fees, earn more interest, and are able to bank from anywhere! Although we both currently use local banks, we also have savings accounts with ING for ourselves and each of our kids (the bank occasionally runs specials where they offer bonuses for opening accounts for your kids). The benefit of moving your savings account or emergency fund to a separate bank is that it takes longer to transfer the money into your regular account, which makes you think twice about doing it.

Emergency Fund

An emergency fund is a savings account for, well, emergencies. Financial advisers recommend keeping enough money in an emergency fun to cover at least three to six months of expenses. Separate from your other savings accounts, this money isn't for vacations, new cars, or Christmas, but really for true emergencies. We know setting aside that much money can be overwhelming to think about if you don't currently have any money in savings, but start by setting aside a small amount each week and celebrate the smaller milestones—the first $100, the first $1,000, etc.—along the way.

Envelope Budgeting

"Envelope budgeting" is a term used for a cash-based budget system where you literally fill envelopes with set amounts of cash for categories like gas, groceries, dining out, etc. When you use all of the cash in one envelope, you can choose to stop spending or to take money out of another envelope, but once the cash is gone, it's gone until the next pay period. This works because you can physically see how much money is going out and/or is left in your envelope, which forces you to pay attention to your spending habits. It can be an eye-opening experience and will encourage you to shop more frugally and think twice before making a purchase. Read more about this idea in *The Total Money Makeover* by Dave Ramsey (http://allingood time.net/totalmoneymakeover).

Sinking Funds

"Sinking funds" refer to savings accounts that you establish for specific savings goals. With a sinking fund, you set aside money to pay for expenses that are regular but may not occur on a monthly basis—things like insurance payments, gifts, vacation, etc. By setting aside money on a regular basis, you have a reserve to draw from when these events pop up. It also enables you to budget for these less frequent expenses on a monthly basis rather than trying to come up with a lump sum all at once.

Pay Yourself First

When you hear people say "pay yourself first" in relation to personal finance, they literally mean pay yourself first. Before you pay your electric bill, before you buy groceries, before you put gas in your car, you first pay yourself by making a regular deposit into a savings account. How much you pay varies greatly depending on your financial situation, but the important thing is that you're establishing the act of saving as a priority and forcing yourself to budget out of your remaining funds. Of course, your second step should be to pay all of your monthly obligations and *then* budget for Starbucks, manicures, and other luxuries out of the remaining amount.

Preventing Identity Theft

Identity theft isn't just a temporary inconvenience; it can be costly and time-consuming as well. If your identity has been stolen, it's important to file a police report, file a report with the FTC, make sure all of your accounts have been closed and reopened, and notify all three credit agencies. But you can avoid all of that by taking some simple precautions to protect yourself:

- Always shred sensitive documents rather than just throwing them away.
- Have account statements, new checks, and other sensitive mail sent to a secure post office box rather than your unlocked mailbox. You can opt out of prescreened offers at 1-888-5-OPT-OUT to reduce the chance of someone claiming one of these on your behalf.
- Keep a list of all of your account numbers and phone numbers so that you can quickly contact customer service if they're lost or stolen.
- Never give out your Social Security number unless you know and trust the company requesting it, and they have a valid reason for doing so.
- Don't throw receipts away in public trash cans.
- Use strong passwords on the Internet that are a combination of letters, numbers, and special characters.
- Request your free credit report once a year from Annual-CreditReport.com to check for any fraudulent activity.

CELL PHONES

The best time to buy a cell phone is when you're not under contract because you'll receive the biggest incentives on a new phone when you sign a new service contract. To really save money, avoid upgrading your phone every one to two years, even if your service provider offers you a special deal for signing an extension on your contract, so that you have the flexibility to cancel or change carriers if needed.

When purchasing a phone without a new contract, you're not likely to find much of a price break. However, purchasing refurbished phones or secondhand phones can net you quite a bit of savings. Too bad Tara didn't have those options available when she dropped her iPhone in the toilet as she was packing to catch a flight for a business engagement . . .

To choose the best cell-phone plan for your family, first check to see which providers offer the best coverage for your area. After that, compare plans between available providers. Which plan works best will vary based on your usage and data needs, but you can use a site like BillShrink.com to easily estimate the costs of various plans across various providers.

Smartphones are all the rage these days, but for most people they're a luxury and not a necessity. Before upgrading to a smartphone, be sure to think through all of the costs, including a monthly data plan (most, but not all, smartphones require them), protective cases, replacement from wear and tear, etc.

For many people, a prepaid cell phone is still a great option. If the only reason you're getting a cell phone is for emergencies, consider loading a prepaid with the minimum amount of minutes as insurance rather than using a cell phone every day.

TIP: Every year, Americans discard more than 125 million cell phones, which accounts for nearly 65,000 tons of toxic waste. Most of these are still in working order, and even those that aren't can be refurbished and recycled. There are several ways to recycle old cell phones. Donate them to CellPhonesfor Soldiers.com, the National Coalition Against Domestic Violence (NCADV.org), or Phones4Life.org. If you have a newer-model phone and are looking to recoup some of your cost of upgrading, you can sell it on eBay or participate in store recycling programs, which often reward you with gift cards. If your phone is really done and ready to be recycled, many stores such as Best Buy, cell-phone carriers, and office supply stores will recycle it for you free of charge.

COLLEGE

While we both have four-year bachelor's degrees (Tara in fine arts, Mandi in business administration), neither of us believes in forcing kids to go if they don't want to go for themselves. We expect that our kids will pay at least a portion of their college expenses to help them stay invested in their education. And if college doesn't seem to be the right fit for them, then we'll help them look for other opportunities.

College Tuition

Outside of applying for as many scholarships and grants as possible, there are a few ways you can save on college tuition by being proactive. Consider taking advanced placement (aka AP) courses in high school. You can then attempt to "test out" of some of the prerequisite courses in college and move on to the more advanced courses immediately. The tests can also be taken without the classes, but because each test costs between $77 and $150 (depending on college registration fees), you'll want to be sure you have a good grasp of the material before registering for the test.

Many schools also offer joint enrollment programs where you can take college courses for both high school and college credit. This option is often a better choice than AP courses since you're guaranteed credit and your fees and books are usually included as part of the program.

For college students looking to offset the costs of college, work/study programs give you the opportunity to earn money by working on campus during the school year. You won't get rich, but you will be able to cover your books and some of your other expenses.

As a general rule, public universities are less expensive than private institutions. While most online institutions are more expensive than state universities, many colleges offer online programs these days.

Mandi began her college career by taking four CLEP (College Level Examination Program) tests to earn twelve credits. She attended a local community college for the first two years and then completed her degree through the University of

Maryland University College online program. By completing her degree online, she saved on the cost of room and board as well as the expense of commuting back and forth. Online classes also gave her the flexibility to work full-time while studying for her degree, and because UMUC is a public institution, her education cost significantly less than many of her peers'.

Ohio State offered a joint enrollment program at Tara's high school to qualifying juniors and seniors. She didn't learn about the program until the end of her junior year, but she applied and was accepted for her senior year. Her tuition, class fees, supplies, and textbooks were all covered under the program, and when she graduated from high school, she had earned enough credits to enroll in college as a sophomore, saving her a full year of tuition.

The best time for your high school student to begin thinking about college is during his or her junior year so that there is plenty of time to consider various colleges and prepare for the application and admission requirements. Some students may start as early as sophomore year in order to take advantage of early decision programs, but there's no real need to start before junior year for most students.

Before applying, students will need their SAT and/or ACT scores, letters of recommendation, and a list of all of the requirements for each school they want to apply to. Applications can be sent as early as November of their senior year, and it can take a few months to get everything together, so don't put off starting for too long.

Schedule college tours during spring of a student's junior year or fall of their senior year. However, keep in mind that admissions offices may be too busy to meet during April and May when they're reviewing applications. It's best to select a daytime visit while classes are in full session, preferably Monday through Thursday, as fewer classes are offered on Fridays.

Textbooks

To save on college textbooks, buy used, or borrow or share the textbooks you need whenever possible. These days you can also rent textbooks online through sites like Rent-A-Text.com. Be sure to ask professors if an older edition of the textbook is acceptable since the price drops significantly when a new edition is released. Some professors will require students to have the latest edition, but many will be flexible in this area.

COMPUTERS

We'll admit that we both love technology, and since we've been working at home—primarily over the Internet—for more than eight years, we've had quite a few computers between us. In general, the best times to buy a new computer are January, April, July, and October as new models are released. However, you'll also find great deals during back-to-school season in August and September as well as around all of the national "shopping" holidays.

TIP: If you're looking to save money on a computer, consider buying a refurbished computer, which are often just as reliable as a brand-new one. Unless you are working with a ton of files or programs, you probably don't need the biggest hard drive or the most memory that manufacturers offer. In general, laptops are more portable and convenient but won't last as long as desktops. In fact, Mandi has an old Dell desktop that she's had for ten years. It doesn't really compare to today's technology, but it still works in a pinch!

Extended Warranty

You probably won't need an extended warranty for a desktop since it doesn't wear out the same way a laptop does and any defects will be noticeable within the original warranty period, but you may want to consider an extended warranty on a laptop. Be sure to price-compare with third-party warranty providers such as SquareTrade.com. For laptops that will get a lot of use, you may also consider adding accidental damage coverage, which covers drops, spills, and more even when you're at fault.

To protect your computer against viruses and spyware, install a reliable antivirus software such as Norton, McAfee, or AVG. There are rebate offers on Norton and McAfee all the time, and AVG has a free version of their program available for download.

Computer Backups

If you've ever experienced the "blue screen of death" on your computer, you know the feeling of panic and how images of all the precious photos and important documents you have stored on it flash through your mind! You *need* to have a system in place to make sure your files are backed up, and if you don't yet have one, you need to get one, preferably today or this week at the very least.

You can certainly back up with CDs or DVDs, but with the increasing size of photos, you may end up with a large number of discs to organize and keep track of.

Here are two other options for backing up your files:

- Dropbox. Mandi uses Dropbox (http://allingoodtime.net/dropbox) not just to back up her files on a remote server but also to access them from multiple computers and devices so that she can always have access to those files, no matter where she is. They also offer a public folder that allows you to share large files with anyone you want over the Internet. Dropbox offers all users 2 GB of space free, with opportunities to increase your storage space by sharing the service. For Apple devotees, iCloud is a free service that makes managing data across multiple devices super easy (http://allingoodtime.net/icloud)!

- External hard drives. External hard drives give you the ability to back up your files offline with much more available space than a CD or DVD. You'll pay more up front, but you can find external drives that can hold several terabytes of files, which is more than enough for most people.

COUPONS & REBATES

Using coupons can save you quite a bit on your groceries and household items (more about this in the Kitchen section), but the key to effectively using coupons is organizing them in a way that makes them easy to use. There are three main methods that avid couponers use:

Binder Method
With the binder method, you clip all of the coupons that you get from newspaper inserts or the Internet and organize them in a large binder using baseball-card inserts by category. This looks great and makes it supereasy to see all of your coupons, but it's time-consuming and carrying a bulky binder can be a hassle.

Coupon Box
Some couponers opt for a coupon box instead. They still clip all of their coupons, but they file them by category in a box rather than folding and fitting them into the baseball-card holders. This is a faster way to do it, but you lose the benefit of being able to see all of your coupons at once, which makes it harder to find individual coupons.

Insert Method
An alternative to both of those methods is the insert method, where you simply file your inserts by date without clipping any coupons. Before a trip to the store, you go through and clip the coupons you need to take with you. The downside of this method is you may miss savings opportunities by not having all of your coupons with you at all times.

Tara uses a hybrid method for her coupons. She clips coupons for items that she buys regularly or brands that she loves and files them in a Couponizer (http://allingoodtime.net/couponizer) that fits easily in her purse. She also files any free product coupons that she receives by mail as well as her printable coupons. Then she files the rest of the insert in case a good deal comes up so that she can quickly find those additional coupons.

Rebates

You can save a lot of money by participating in rebate programs, but the tricky part is keeping track of all of your outstanding rebates. RebateTracker.com is a free service that lets you organize your rebates, track those that are outstanding, and receive reminders as due dates approach. Be sure to read the fine print on all rebate offers, as many of them now offer gift cards rather than cash, so you may only be able to use your rebate at a specific retailer or during a specific time period.

CREDIT-CARD DEBT

The best time to pay off your credit card is in full each month in order to avoid interest charges that can add up over time. However, if you're not able to do this, we recommend scheduling your payment as soon as your statement arrives (even if you schedule it for the due date several weeks out) so that it doesn't get missed, which can result in hefty late fees.

There is some debate about the best way to pay off larger amounts of credit-card debt. Some experts recommend paying off the debts with the highest interest rates first while just paying the minimums on the other balances regardless of the amount you owe on each. Other experts, like Dave Ramsey, recommend the debt snowball, where you focus on paying off your smallest balance first. As you pay off each debt, you apply the money you were putting toward that one to the next highest balance and so on until your debts are paid in full. The benefit of this system is that you have the satisfaction of feeling like actual progress is being made as you close out old debts and you gain momentum as you go.

We've both used the debt snowball method to pay off our debt after first trying the more conventional method of paying off the highest interest rate first, which can be discouraging because you don't see a lot of real progress, especially if your highest-interest-rate debt is also your largest. With a snowball, we found that the satisfaction of paying off our smaller debts in full felt like a much bigger success and kept us on track to pay off all of our debts.

How to Get a Live Agent When Calling Customer Service

There's nothing more frustrating than getting stuck in a perpetual loop when trying to call customer service. "Please press one . . . please press three . . . please say the reason for your call . . . I'm sorry, I can't understand you. Please start over." Here are a few tips to help you bypass the computer systems and get to a live person more quickly:

- Press the 0 key several times.
- Don't respond to the commands.

- Press # or *.
- When responding to the voice-prompt systems, say "customer service," "agent," "associate," or "representative."
- Use a site like GetHuman.com to find the actual steps to get a live person for more than two thousand companies.

DIGITAL CAMERAS

The best time to buy a digital camera is right after the newest models are released, which happens as often as twice a year these days. If you can find the previous model still in stock, you'll be able to pick it up at a significant discount with very few differences in features. Mandi and her husband purchased a Sony DSLR for just $250 at Target just weeks before their youngest daughter was born because they picked up the floor model (which was in perfect condition) just as the sales associates were getting ready to switch out the models. Camera accessories are often priced as loss leaders during the holidays to draw consumers into electronics or big-box stores, and you'll often find sales on these accessories at Amazon.com as well.

EMAIL

Both of us use and love Gmail for all of our email needs. Gmail is an Internet-based email server, which means you can access all of your emails from anywhere with an Internet connection.

If you use a desktop client such as Outlook, or a smartphone or mobile device, you can also download your emails to those while still keeping your online backup. Gmail's basic free service offers a huge amount of storage, which means you can archive your emails for later reference without worrying about a full in-box bouncing new messages back to the sender.

ESTATE PLANNING

Wills are one of those things that no one really wants to think about, but they are so incredibly important. When is the best time to make one? If you don't have one, now is the best time. The ramifications of not having one are greater than just ensuring who gets what property. Even in clear-cut cases where the beneficiary is obvious, not having a will can be a financial nightmare since all property without a clear directive must legally go through probate. This is a task that is all too often pushed aside in the busyness of everyday life, and while chances are that you won't ever need these things, the risk of not having them is too big to take that chance. Anyone can write their own will, but it's best to have an attorney review it to proofread and look for loose ends. For a sobering look at some of the consequences of not taking time to fully think through these issues, we recommend *Wear Clean Underwear!: A Fast, Fun, Friendly and Essential Guide to Legal Planning for Busy Parents* by Alexis Martin Neely (http://allingoodtime.net/estateplanning).

TIP: Name legal guardians for your kids *today* with the free online tool at KidsProtectionPlan.com.

FILE CABINETS

There's not really a best time to purchase a filing cabinet, but you'll save time and money by purchasing the right one for your needs. For example, you may consider scanning documents and storing them digitally rather than in a file cabinet, or you can reduce the amount of space you need by keeping only those documents that you have to rather than every piece of paper that comes into your home.

To organize your paper files, divide your records by category and then again by subcategory. For example, insurance documents would be one category, with car insurance, homeowner's insurance, and health insurance as subcategories. Medical records, school records, and utilities may be additional categories, depending on your situation. See Mandi's file system at work at http://allingoodtime.net/filing.

How Long to Keep Records and Documents

With the advent of the digital age, we can now access a lot of our records online and no longer need to keep paper records. If you use a budgeting system like Microsoft Money or Mint .com, where you keep detailed transaction records, you can probably get rid of most of your paper records. If you don't have this kind of digital backup, you may want to keep records for the current year in case you need to refer back to them for tax purposes.

THINGS YOU DON'T NEED TO KEEP:

- utility records
- bank statements
- credit-card bills
- older insurance policies
- pay stubs
- receipts

THINGS YOU NEED TO KEEP:

- annual investment statements
- loan documents
- warranty documentation for large purchases
- savings bonds
- vehicle records
- defined-benefit plan documents
- estate planning documents
- current insurance policies
- tax returns

GIFT CARDS

The best time to buy gift cards directly from retailers is before Christmas, when you'll often find specials that give you bonuses for buying a certain number of gift cards. However, you'll find the best deals after Christmas from gift-card resellers like GiftCards.com or eBay. You can also sell gift cards through these sites if you receive one that you won't use. You probably won't get the full value, but you'll get more than you'd get by leaving it in your wallet for two years!

TIP: When you use a gift card, use a pen to write the remaining balance on the card so that you always know how much is available.

GREETING CARDS

At $3 to $4 a card, the cost of sending greeting cards to your friends and family for birthdays, anniversaries, and other occasions can quickly add up! You'll find inexpensive greeting cards at the dollar store, and you'll also find occasional coupons as well as sales at drugstores. Trader Joe's offers a great selection of $0.99 cards for various occasions. And Hallmark has released high-value coupons in the November and December issues of many magazines for the past several years, and you could use these to stock up on greeting cards for the year. You'll also find that many of the popular photo sites (http://allingoodtime.net/photoprints) offer free custom photo cards, which you can customize for any occasion or need, or even create all-purpose cards to use as needed.

INSURANCE

Life Insurance

Life insurance is an important consideration for every family, especially families with children to care for. The death of a parent (or, God forbid, both parents) is devastating enough without worrying about finances and how to make ends meet. Life insurance premiums are lower the younger and healthier you are, so lock in your rate early for a more affordable plan. Although you want to be sure your family is taken care of in case of your death, buying a $1 million plan may not be necessary and will unnecessarily raise your premiums. You'll also want to check to see whether paying your bill annually rather than monthly reduces your fees. Your health also plays a role in your rate, and while we don't recommend waiting to get insurance, you'll get better rates if you're healthy and don't smoke or drink excessively.

Homeowner's or Renter's Insurance

Homeowner's insurance is required by most insurance companies, but even if you own your home outright, you'll want to protect your investment with adequate insurance that covers the structure as well as your belongings. Although you don't need to cover the structure if you're renting, renter's insurance covers the contents of your home in case of damage or loss. To reduce your insurance premium, consider a higher deductible as long as you can afford to pay it. Most companies also offer a discount when you purchase your homeowner's or renter's insurance from the same company as your auto insurance, but you should also compare these quotes with any plans available through alumni associations or other groups. Finally, a monitored security system can decrease your premium, and you may also be able to get a discount if yours is a nonsmoking household.

TIP: Although we hope you never need to take advantage of your homeowner's or renter's insurance, having a detailed home inventory can make a significant difference if you do. Take time to carefully document your electronics, valuables, and to take pictures or videos of the contents of your home. Some plans include limits on electronics, jewelry, and other valuables, and you may need a rider to properly cover these items. Use this printable home inventory to get started: (http://allingoodtime.net/homeinventory).

MORTGAGES

Anytime you make additional payments to the principal owed on your home, you're cutting interest and time off of your mortgage. However, this can be negated by the many fees that your lender probably wants to charge to set up this service for you. Instead, make these payments on your own by indicating that they are to be applied to the principal owed. Whether you make them bimonthly, pay one-twelfth of a payment a month on top of your regular payment, or just make an extra payment every year, you're still ultimately achieving the same results.

PIGGY BANKS

Saving change and small bills is an easy way to save up for special treats over time. Tara's family has a large watercooler jug into which they toss all of their loose change and a few dollars a month. They save it up and then empty it out to pay for a special family treat.

If you have a lot of change and don't want to spend a lot of time rolling it, the Coinstar machines that you find in lots of grocery stores these days are an excellent alternative. They charge a small fee for redeeming your change for cash, but if you opt for a gift card instead, the fee is waived. Even better, they occasionally offer special promotions where you'll receive a bonus gift card when redeeming your change!

Swag Bucks (http://allingoodtime.net/swagbucks) is a virtual piggy bank of sorts. Use the Swag Bucks search engine for all of your Internet searches and earn Swag Bucks that you can redeem for prizes and gift cards. Our favorite rewards are the Amazon.com gift cards, which you can use for everything from diapers and food to books and special treats.

PHOTOS

Many people buy photo printers, ink, and paper only to discover that printing at home doesn't actually save you money. Photo printing companies regularly offer free or discounted prints at an unbeatable price, and while you can't really beat the convenience of being able to print at home, as long as you plan ahead, having them printed and mailed to you is the least expensive option.

You'll also find tons of free photo gifts, especially around the major holidays (Valentine's Day, Mother's and Father's Day, and Christmas). You shouldn't ever have to pay full price for photo gifts such as mugs, calendars, and plates since there are so many deals available. We've put together a full list of photo companies at http://allingoodtime.net/photoprints.

If you take a lot of digital pictures (Mandi has saved more than twenty thousand of the countless pictures she's taken since she started having kids), it's important to organize them in a way that makes them easy to find. Mandi organizes hers by date, but at some point she'd like to go through and tag them all so that she still knows who's who in fifty years! If you use Windows, the Windows Live Photo Gallery includes a tagging tool that automatically embeds the tags in your photos.

TIP: We can't stress enough how important it is to regularly back up your photos. We know more than one person who's been devastated by the loss of irreplaceable family photos because they didn't have them backed up. Burn them to a CD, use a third-party backup tool (such as one of those listed in the sidebar on page 146), or upload them to a site like Flickr. Or do all three to be really safe!

POSTAGE & SHIPPING

Save money on postage by signing up for automatic billing or bill pay through your bank, and use online sites like Facebook and Evite for event invitations. When mailing books, CDs, or other media, use media mail, which is slower (though not usually as slow as they estimate, in our experience) but also much less expensive than other mail services. For most packages, first-class mail is the least expensive way to go. However, if you want your package shipped faster or you're concerned about reliability, FedEx or UPS is probably a better choice since you'll get detailed tracking information and they have lower incidences of damaged or lost packages.

The best time to go to the post office is early in the morning. You want to avoid the lunchtime and evening rush, when they're guaranteed to be busy and backed up. If a postal rate hike is on the horizon, consider purchasing Freedom stamps. You can purchase any quantity at the current postal rates, but their value will increase with future rate hikes, saving you a little extra cash.

Resources for Work-at-Home Opportunities

We've both worked from home for many years in a variety of job positions, including call-center work, legal coding, transcription, and blogging. Working from home takes time, initiative, and hard work, but it's also extremely rewarding.

The most important thing to keep in mind is that many work-at-home opportunities are scams. It's a sad but true fact that there are many people on the Internet who earn a living by scamming other people. But there are plenty of legitimate opportunities as well! Avoid scams by following these three rules:

1. Never pay for the opportunity to work at home. The only exception to this is for home party businesses such as Usborne Books or Pampered Chef, where you receive a high-value kit to help kick-start your business.

2. Envelope-stuffing jobs are scams. Every one of them, every time. The envelopes being stuffed are being sent to convince other people to sign up to do the same thing.
3. Legitimate data-entry jobs are very hard to come by. Never pay for an opportunity to do data entry, no matter what reason they give you.

In general, follow your gut and ask around if an opportunity seems too good to be true!

Our favorite resources for legitimate opportunities are listed below:

- WAHM.com
- WorkPlaceLikeHome.com

You'll find tons of information and experiences to help you sort through available opportunities and improve your skills.

PRINTING

If you regularly use your printer—for printable coupons, home-schooling work sheets, or any other reason—you've probably cringed over the cost of a new printer cartridge once or twice. The best time to buy a new printer is with a new computer, since many companies offer special promotions when you buy both. You'll also find great deals on printers during the back-to-school and Christmas shopping seasons. Before you buy a printer, though, always check the cost of replacement ink in relation to the estimated number of pages it prints so that you're not surprised by the cost the first time you need to buy it.

You can purchase refilled inkjet cartridges for significantly less than the original cartridges, but we've had iffy results with these cartridges and mostly stick with new name-brand cartridges these days.

TIP: Save money on actual printing costs by setting your printer to draft mode, which saves as much as half of the ink you'll use on the regular setting. Also print in black and white unless you actually need the color for whatever you're printing. To save on paper, watch for rebate offers through office supply stores' reward programs to purchase paper for as low as free.

Like other electronics, be sure to plug your printer into a power strip that you can turn off when not in use to prevent vampire power usage. IGo also offers a line of power-saving surge protectors that automatically turn off when a device is not in use (http://allingoodtime.net/igo).

RETURNS

The best time to make a store return is early in the morning and within the posted return policy of the store. The worst time? The day after Christmas, of course! Be prepared with tags and receipts if available to make your return process as smooth as possible.

TIP: As moms of nine children with varying rates of growth and tastes, we greatly appreciate finding gift receipts tucked in with gifts. We hate hassling the gift giver when an item doesn't fit quite right or when one of our girls suddenly decides that purple is in fact her favorite color now and she wants nothing to do with the pink Barbie she received.

SAFES

A small fireproof lockbox is an item that every family should own. Keep your important paperwork, like birth certificates, Social Security cards, passports, titles, etc., in it for protection in the event of a fire. This is also the ideal place to keep irreplaceable photos and jewelry. Upgrade to a larger fireproof floor safe if you have a large quantity of paperwork or other items and need the additional space.

SHREDDERS

Sensitive documents and old credit and debit cards should always be shredded before disposing of them for protection from identity theft. Look for a model that shreds with a crosscut for the most security. You can pick these up at big-box stores like Walmart and Target, for a reasonable price.

We recommend keeping these unplugged when they're not in use because they're a magnet for little kids. Tara made the mistake of leaving hers plugged in once and ended up losing several unpaid bills and a free Doritos coupon to a curious toddler.

TAXES

There are a couple of benefits to preparing your taxes earlier rather than waiting until the April 15 deadline. If you're due a refund, the sooner you file, the sooner you'll receive your check. If, on the other hand, you owe money, you'll have more time to get that money together.

One thing to keep in mind is that if you often get large refunds from the IRS, you're letting the government use your money for free, and you're missing out on the interest you could be earning with a savings account. We know that there are benefits to letting the government "hold" your money so that you get an extra bonus check once a year, but if you want to maximize your money, adjust your tax withholding and send the extra money into a sinking fund instead.

Many people do their own taxes to save money, and while we've both done our own taxes for many years, you may want to consider hiring a tax professional to make sure you're taking advantage of all available deductions or to help you navigate complicated tax issues. If you're comfortable doing your own taxes, we recommend online services such as TaxACT, Turbo-Tax, and H&R Block (http://allingoodtime.net/taxsoftware), all of which walk you through a series of questions and then automatically populate the forms you need and calculate your tax obligation to make sure you don't miss anything.

TIP: To simplify your tax preparation process, use the checklist in the sidebar to gather all of the necessary documents. Then prepare for next year by creating a folder for all of the receipts and documents you receive throughout the year.

Checklist of Tax Documents

Use this basic list of tax documents to begin gathering records for yourself or your tax preparer:

PERSONAL:
- Social Security numbers
- child-care provider information

EMPLOYMENT & INCOME:
- employment income (W-2)
- miscellaneous income (1099s, etc.)
- state and local income tax refunds
- investment income and expenses

MORTGAGE & RENTAL:
- address(es)
- mortgage interest (1098)
- sale of real estate (1099-S)
- real-estate taxes
- rent paid
- moving expenses

SELF-EMPLOYMENT:
- income records (1099-MISC)
- business expense records
- taxes paid
- home-office deduction records (deductions)
- charitable gifts
- qualifying volunteer expenses

- qualifying job expenses
- child-care expenses
- medical expenses
- adoption expenses
- alimony paid
- tax-return preparation fees

If you have a home business, you may want to use an accordion file that allows you to organize receipts, income, and other information separately so that it's easy to sort through at tax time.

Stop Unwanted Junk Mail

Joshua Becker from BecomingMinimalist.com shared these tips for reducing the amount of unwanted junk mail you receive:

1. Register on DMAChoice.org's "do not mail" list.
2. Opt out of preapproved credit-card, mortgage, and insurance offers at OptOutScreening.com.
3. Remove your name from Abacus, an alliance of catalog and publishing companies, by sending an email to *abacusoptout@epsilon.com* with your full name (including middle initial) and complete address.
4. Call the number on the back of any catalogs you receive and ask to be removed from their mailing list.
5. Contact local organizations such as charities, local organizations, and alumni lists to ask to be removed.

Organize with the Cozi Online Organizer

Cozi.com is a popular online organizer that allows you to create a family calendar, shared shopping lists, to-do lists, and a family journal, all of which you can access from your computer or mobile phone. What makes Cozi really great, though, is the ability to share calendars with other members of your family, text shopping lists, and set up automatic email reminders!

Kitchen

APPLIANCES

Like washing machines and dryers, new appliance models are typically released in September and October, and you'll also find significant discounts during holiday sales. Look for scratch-and-dent models that you can pick up for much less than their "perfect" counterparts, since many times these scratches and dents are barely noticeable. Be sure to consider the energy costs of running your appliance. You may pay more for a more efficient refrigerator but quickly recoup the cost in your power savings. Don't be afraid to haggle on the price, and be sure to ask about free installation service. You'll also find gently used appliances on Craigslist at a fraction of the cost of new appliances.

Cleaning
Chest Freezer
The buildup of frost inside your chest freezer can make it less efficient over time. Defrost your chest freezer once a year or when there's more than a quarter-inch worth of frost built up on the sides. To easily defrost your freezer, move all of the contents to another freezer or pack them in an insulated cooler. Turn off the freezer and open the lid to let it warm up. If you need to do it more quickly, you can boil water in a large pot and set it on a towel inside the freezer and then shut the door to allow the steam to melt the frost. You may need to replace the steaming water several times, but it will melt much more quickly than if you just wait for it to melt naturally.

Countertops
It's important to disinfect your countertops regularly, especially after you've worked with raw meat. For a frugal and non-toxic disinfectant, spray your counters with vinegar and then wipe them dry. Although this will kill a lot of the germs and bacteria by itself, you can be extra sure by following it with spraying the countertops with hydrogen peroxide and allowing it to air-dry.

Microwave
Cleaning your microwave is as simple as microwaving a cup of water for about five minutes. When it's done, the inside should be nice and steamy, and wiping out the grime inside will be practically effortless! Take this quick tip one step further to freshen your house up in the process. In the spring and sum-

mer, Tara likes to add a bit of citrus juice to the water, and in the fall and winter she adds a few drops of pure vanilla extract. You'll have a clean microwave, and your home will smell delicious.

Remove burned odors from the microwave by mixing two tablespoons of ground coffee with one-half cup of water. Microwave for three minutes, and the smell should be gone!

Oven

Self-cleaning ovens work by burning off food particles at a high temperature. Although these ovens usually have a safety feature to prevent you from opening the door while they're cleaning to reduce the risk of burns, the outside can still get pretty hot, so it's important to keep kids away from them while in use.

If you have to clean your oven manually, try this homemade cleaner we found in *Whole Living* magazine. Mix two cups baking soda, one cup washing soda, one teaspoon dish soap, and one tablespoon white vinegar until they form a paste. Then apply thickly to the sides and bottom of your oven and let sit overnight. In the morning, use a wet cloth to scrub the sides until they're clean. Although this is a nontoxic cleaner, you'll still want to wear gloves while you use it!

Refrigerator/Freezer

Clean out your refrigerator each week *before* you grocery shop. Throw away old food, wipe shelves, and reorganize what's left. Not only will it be easier to put away the groceries when you get home, but you'll have to deep-clean less often if you're wiping the shelves every week (and it really only takes ten to fifteen minutes to do). Every few months, be sure to vacuum the refrigerator vent and coils to keep it running more efficiently. Keep an open box of baking soda in your fridge to keep odors at bay.

Sponges

Kitchen sponges can be used for a variety of tasks such as washing dishes, wiping the counters, and cleaning up small spills. But while sponges are handy and convenient, it's often said that the average kitchen sponge is the biggest source of germs in the entire house. Protect your family from the spread of germs and other bacteria with one of these three methods:

1. Wet your sponge and pop it in the microwave for two minutes. Be careful because it will be very hot when it's finished, so let it sit for a while.
2. If you run your dishwasher on a hot cycle, stick your sponge in when you run it.
3. Wash your sponges in the laundry with your other rags, using bleach and hot water. You can run them through the dryer, but they'll last longer if you pull them out and let them air-dry.

No matter which method you use, it's important to change and wash your sponges every one to two days. They may wear out a little faster from running through a hot wash, but if you buy good-quality sponges, they should still last for six to twelve months, and you won't have to worry about spreading germs around in the meantime!

Toaster

Dirty, crumb-filled toasters are not only inefficient; they're also a fire hazard. Clean your toaster easily in these five easy steps:

1. Unplug the unit and make sure that it is completely cool. Yes, this should go without saying, but, well, it needs to be said.
2. Remove the crumb tray from the bottom of the appliance and wash it in hot, soapy water. Rinse and dry thoroughly.
3. Tip the toaster over a garbage can and give it a good shake to dislodge crumbs.
4. Wipe down the outside of the appliance, and then use an old damp toothbrush to scrub any remaining crumbs off and carbon buildup off the heat coils inside the toaster. Shake the debris out over a trash can again.
5. Let the unit dry out completely before plugging it back in.

Recipe for Clorox Anywhere

Although Clorox Anywhere is an indispensable part of Tara's cleaning process, she couldn't bring herself to shell out $3.29 a bottle for something that is 99.9905% water after her product samples ran out. She did a little fancy math to convert the percentages of water and bleach to useful quantities and came up with this simple recipe:

- 1 1/2 teaspoons of bleach
- 22 oz. water

Fill spray bottle with water and then add bleach. Put the nozzle on the bottle and shake gently to mix.

COOK DINNER

Cooking dinner can be a time-consuming task, which is one of the reasons why so many of us end up eating out or grabbing fast food on the way home. Preparing home-cooked meals will save you a significant amount of money, though, and there are ways to do it without adding more to your daily to-do list:

- Use the Crock-Pot. Start your meal in the morning and let it cook all day. Your house will smell great and dinner will be ready and waiting for you at the end of the day.

- Stock your freezer. Mandi has stocked her freezer with six weeks of meals before the birth of her last two babies, and being able to pull them out of the freezer each day rather than having to make them from scratch has been a huge time-saver, especially since her last daughter was very colicky. Although Mandi really only does this when she's expecting, there are many people who did it regularly, through a method called once-a-month cooking. Visit OnceaMonthMom.com for ready-to-go meal plans and step-by-step instructions.

Family Dinners

The research shows that eating together as a family lays an important foundation for healthy childhood development. Encourage conversation at the dinner table by asking questions (for example, "What was the best part of your day? The worst?"), or pick up a set of conversation starters for fun topics. Mandi's family has a set of these, and her daughters beg for them at the dinner table even though they've already been through all of the questions several times.

- Another way to stock your freezer is by simply making extra each time you cook a meal. When you're cooking cubed chicken or ground beef, double or triple your batch and freeze the extras. Next time you make lasagna or another casserole, prepare two at the same time and stick one in the freezer. It really doesn't take that much more effort to make two, and you'll be thankful that you did it the next time you want a break from cooking!

COOKWARE

According to the Cookware Manufacturers Association, the best times to buy cookware are in April and May in anticipation of graduations and weddings and in October and November for the holidays.

DISHES

Target has a great selection of midpriced dishes, and they rotate their colors and styles frequently, so you can pick up a great set on clearance for a steal. Mandi got a set of lime-green dishes this way when her family moved to their new home. Because they were on clearance, she bought extras as replacements since she knew they would inevitably break some over the years and they wouldn't be able to buy replacements. Unfortunately, she couldn't find extras of all of the pieces in the set, so she had Tara shop for some at her local store as well. It was a great plan except that it was more than two years before they remembered to exchange them when they got together!

Many people prefer Corelle dinnerware because it is break- and chip-resistant. Mandi's uncle learned the hard way that that doesn't mean they're unbreakable when he demonstrated their strength by dropping one of her grandmother's plates on the ground, and it shattered into a million tiny pieces.

If you are looking for higher-end dish sets, be sure to check the warehouse seconds rooms at the plants where they're made. Before they had kids, Tara and her husband used to head to the Fiestaware plant to hunt down rare colors in their seconds room. Although these items are technically flawed, many times the flaws are barely noticeable.

Although we tend to think of hand-washing dishes as the old-fashioned, frugal way, most dishwashers today are actually more efficient at washing dishes. Run your dishwasher at night, especially if your power company charges a premium during the day, and turn off the heated dry to save electricity.

Homemade Dish Detergent

If you're looking to reduce the amount of chemicals in your home and save money, try this homemade dish detergent from Alyssa Francis:

Mix equal parts borax and baking soda. Add two tablespoons of the mixture to each load of dishes. If you're worried about streaking or spotting, use vinegar as a rinse aid in your dishwasher.

Be sure to rinse your dishes thoroughly before putting them in the dishwasher since this cleaner may not be as effective at getting hard food off of your dishes because it doesn't contain the chemicals of traditional detergents.

FARMERS' MARKET

Although farmers' markets aren't always less expensive than the grocery store (sometimes they're even more expensive), there are ways to save money at these places as well. One of the best things you can do is develop relationships with the farmers. They'll be more likely to offer you a deal if you have a genuine relationship! Once you have done this, you'll be able to ask for discounts on surplus produce or arrange for bulk purchases that you can split with family and friends. Remember that you'll find the best selection first thing in the morning and the best prices right at closing. For more sources for fresh produce, see the sidebar on page 192.

Produce Wash

Make your own produce wash with one part vinegar, three parts water. Mix in a spray bottle and store under your sink with a produce brush. We recommend using organic vinegar for this since some vinegar is petroleum based, and manufacturers aren't required to disclose this on their labels.

SMALL APPLIANCES

Small appliances are popular as holiday gifts, so you'll find lots of sale pricing in December. After the holidays, you're likely to find some bargains as well, as stores try to off-load any surplus inventory. These days, there's a small appliance for everything—from smoothies and pizzelles to quesadillas and rice. While many of these small appliances save you time in the kitchen, think carefully before buying them since having too many will just leave your kitchen feeling cluttered and make it harder to get to the ones you really do use.

Frugal Stainless-Steel Cleaner

Stainless-steel appliances can be a beautiful addition to a kitchen, but with little ones in the house even "smudge-resistant" brushed stainless steel ends up with streaks and smudges. Stainless-steel cleaner isn't cheap, but you can keep your appliances shiny and smudge-free with baby oil, which also helps guard against fingerprints.

1. Put a small amount of baby oil on a dry rag.
2. Rub it over the surface of the stainless steel in long, even strokes.
3. Buff off the excess baby oil with a second dry cloth. Be sure to get all of the excess baby oil off or it will attract lint.
4. Wipe with a dry cloth whenever you notice smudges or streaks.
5. Repeat every week or two as needed.
6. Occasionally, clean the whole thing with Windex or vinegar to remove any excess oil and then start fresh.

WAREHOUSE MEMBERSHIPS

Warehouse clubs often offer free passes to potential members, so take some time to compare the warehouse clubs in your area before signing up for one. Stretch your membership by stocking up right before your membership expires and waiting four to six weeks to renew, effectively getting you a free month.

One of the dangers of a warehouse membership is the temptation to overbuy. Avoid this by buying the staples you know you'll use rather than every great deal you see. Tara's family uses their warehouse membership to stock up on staples that are priced less in bulk, such as frozen chicken breasts, ground beef, milk, cheese, flour, sugar, etc.

Stock-Up Prices:

- toilet paper, 50 cents per double roll
- paper towels, 75 cents per roll
- baby wipes, 2 cents per wipe
- premium diapers, 22 cents per size 3 diaper (subtract a few cents for smaller size and add a few for larger)
- laundry detergent, 10 cents per ounce
- dishwasher detergent, 10 cents per tab or 5 cents per ounce for powder/gel
- baby food, 25 cents per jar
- cereal, $1 per box
- boneless skinless chicken breasts, $1.99/lb.
- ground beef (80 to 85 percent lean), $1.99/lb.
- boneless pork chops, $1.99/lb.

GROCERIES

We could write a whole book just on saving money on groceries—or Tara could at least—but we'll have to stick with a basic overview here. Many people think that buying generic or store brands will save them the most money, and this is true if you aren't fond of using coupons. Because Mandi's family lives so far out of "town," they prefer to shop at Walmart once a week and use only the very best high-value coupons. They spend approximately $100 a week on their family's groceries and household needs while focusing on cooking from scratch and generic ingredients, which isn't too bad.

However, with just a little effort, you can dramatically cut your grocery budget while purchasing brand-name products. It's all a matter of learning your favorite store's sales cycle. Try keeping a price book for a couple of months every time you make a trip to the store to track the prices of the products you purchase on a regular basis. Most products go on sale approximately once every six weeks, so the key is to save your coupons and buy enough of each product when it's at its lowest price to last you for a six-week period.

Where do you find great coupons? The Sunday newspaper has coupon inserts most weeks, but you will also find coupons at the grocery stores next to certain items, and there are a ton of coupons available online. The Deal Seeking Mom Coupon Database (http://allingoodtime.net/coupondatabase) is a great resource for figuring out if there are coupons available on the items you want. It lists both newspaper insert and printable coupons (as well as those found in magazines and store pamphlets) so that you can find what you're looking for. You can also save the list of coupons in your stash to your Personal Coupon Box for easier tracking.

You might think that you'd spend a lot of time every week scanning the ads, clipping coupons, and making lists, but the truth is there are tons of resources that will do all of this for you—for free! Deal Seeking Mom covers many of the chains nationwide, listing the best deals of the week with a link to the full list to help you plan your trip. These lists include not only the sales prices but the coupon matchups as well so that most of the hard work is done for you.

Families who prefer a more whole-foods diet rather than processed foods may feel like there aren't any coupons available for the items they purchase, but Tara regularly uses coupons for milk, eggs, carrots, spinach, pineapples, and cheese—you just have to look a little harder for them. However, if you can't find a coupon for them, warehouse clubs like Costco are often a good alternative.

Also, don't discount purchasing grocery items online. We've gotten fantastic deals on peanut butter, whole-grain wild rice, Keurig K-Cups, and more on Amazon.com. Amazon offers subscribe-and-save discounts of 15 percent on many items, and you can cancel or adjust your subscription as needed to make sure you don't receive items you don't need. If you can find a trial offer for Amazon Prime (these are available frequently), you'll also receive free two-day shipping.

TIP: When you're grocery shopping with small children, it helps to park near the cart return so that you can quickly load your kids and your groceries and then return the cart without having to walk halfway across the parking lot!

Organize Your Pantry

Having an organized pantry not only feels good and makes grocery shopping and meal preparation easier; it also saves you money!

1. Use lazy Susans or stair-step shelving for your canned goods.
2. Divide your pantry space into categories of food.
3. Arrange food so that it's easy to see.

4. Keep the ingredients you use more frequently at eye level and easily accessible.
5. Rotate and reorganize your pantry every four to six weeks.
6. Keep a pantry inventory and mark items when they start to run low.
7. As you restock your pantry shelves after grocery shopping, rearrange food to keep it organized.

KEEP "PANTRY MEALS" ON HAND
Keep all of the ingredients on hand for your favorite easy-to-prepare meals for weeks when you don't get to the grocery store or don't have time to create more elaborate meals. Group the ingredients in baskets with a copy of the recipe so that you have everything you need right at your fingertips.

In addition to these basic saving strategies, there are also key times of the year when you'll want to purchase certain grocery staples. We've put together a list of these below:

Baking Supplies

November and December are traditionally heavy baking months, so you'll find lots of fantastic deals on pantry staples. Now is the time to stock up for the year (if you have room) on flour, sugar, yeast, spices, chocolate chips, canned pumpkin, and evaporated milk among other baking products. If you're an oatmeal lover, watch for deals on this staple in January, which is National Oatmeal Month.

Bottled Water

The average cost of bottled water is more than $12 a gallon. Considering that most bottled water is unregulated and often comes from plain ol' tap water anyway, this can really add up to a lot of wasted dollars over time. Instead, purchase some reusable bottles and carry your own bottled water with you when you leave the house so that you're less tempted to buy a bottle while you're out!

Canned Food

Canned food sales are pretty common throughout the year, but you'll find especially good deals on canned soup as the weather turns colder in October. Stock up on canned tomatoes and chilies in the weeks leading up to Super Bowl Sunday when stores price them attractively for game-day appetizers.

Cereal

We all know that a box of cereal doesn't last long at all, and the regular prices on cereal are rather shocking considering how many meals they provide! While you'll find sales and coupons for brand-name cereals year-round, the prices will dip especially low in August and September to prepare for back to school. Tara's target price is about $1 per box, and you can easily achieve this at the grocery store with coupons at this time of year. Check the expiration dates on the boxes as you buy them, and you may just be able to stockpile enough at 75 percent off retail or lower to last you through the year.

Cheese

Fortunately, there have been some fantastic sales on cheese over the past few years. There doesn't seem to be a regular pattern to it, but anytime you spot a real bargain on cheese, stock up. It freezes really well (although you may find that blocks become a little crumbly after being frozen and thawed), so there's no need to pay full price for it when you can buy it on sale ahead of time.

If you have more of a deli-cheese kind of palate, buy from the self-serve cases in the store deli. You'll pay a premium for cheese that's sliced to order, and this is essentially the same cheese at a lower price.

Coffee

If you spend a lot on coffee-shop specialty drinks, search the Internet for at-home versions of these recipes so that you can make your own with your favorite brewed coffee. Even if you buy the most expensive beans or grounds, you'll still be saving over a $4 latte!

Frozen Food

March is National Frozen Food Month, so watch for lots of sales on frozen fruits and veggies, as well as pizzas and frozen dinners. Stores often put their chest freezers on sale this time of year as well and offer free frozen foods with the purchase.

Ice Cream

Not surprisingly, you'll find some of the best ice cream deals during the hot summer months of June, July, and August. If you or your kids are fans of the Fla-Vor-Ice Pops (Tara loves the red ones!), many times you'll find the large cases on clearance at the end of the summer, and these will keep indefinitely.

Frozen Treats

Popsicles and ice cream are a staple of childhood, it seems, but they don't have to be expensive! Here are some of our favorite recipes for frozen treats.

POPSICLES:
Buy inexpensive Popsicle molds (you can often find these in the Dollar Spot at Target or at your local dollar store), and make your own Popsicles with whatever you have on hand. We've used pudding, Kool-Aid, yogurt, juice, or leftover smoothies to make Popsicles in a variety of flavors. You can also add berries or sliced fruit once the Popsicle begins to freeze for an extra fun treat. Just be sure to leave a little bit of room at the top for your Popsicles to expand as they freeze.

HEALTHY ONE-INGREDIENT ICE CREAM:
Jules Clancy from TheStoneSoup.com shared this delicious recipe with us. For easy one-ingredient ice cream, simply freeze two bananas. Remove them from the freezer about ten minutes before you're ready to eat them and let them thaw slightly. Then pop them in the food processor or use your immersion blender to create a smooth, creamy texture. Serve immediately. You can play around with different frozen fruits (although some other fruits may need a little sugar as well) to create a delicious, healthy treat!

COFFEE-CAN ICE CREAM:

We got this fun recipe from *ReadyMade Magazine.*

You'll need:

- ½ cup milk
- 1 ½ cup heavy cream
- ½ cup sugar
- 1 teaspoon vanilla extract
- 1-lb. coffee can with lid
- 5-lb. coffee can with lid
- Crushed ice
- 1 cup rock salt or course table salt

Mix the first four ingredients in the smaller coffee can. Put it inside the larger can and pack the sides with the ice and salt. Replace the lid. (If the lid seems loose, be sure to tape it shut so that it doesn't come off.) Roll the can back and forth or around the room, which is a great way to get kids involved while you wait. After twenty to thirty minutes, open the can and serve!

Meat

There are a few strategies you can use to save on meat. Obviously you can watch for sales and stock up at that time, but also make friends with the butcher at your grocer. He'll be able to tell you when they put out their markdowns, which will save you even more. Use these within a few days or freeze them for future use. Also watch for buy-one-get-one-free sales on meat; just be sure to check the price to ensure that your store is not inflating the "regular prices" to make up the difference.

Costco typically has great-quality meat and produce at great prices, and since meat can be frozen, you can take advantage of the bulk price to stock up. Many families also buy "half a cow" from a local beef farm, which is a great option if you eat a lot of red meat, especially if you're looking for local, organic, grass-fed beef.

Hot-dog sales will start in May and last throughout the summer. Hot dogs freeze particularly well, so you can buy several packages to freeze if you want to enjoy them at a bargain over the winter.

Deli meats are also often on sale, but they will be found at the lowest price in August and September with the back-to-school sales.

Produce

Buying your produce based on what's in season will not only net you significant savings, but you'll also enjoy fruits and veggies that are more flavorful and nutrient packed. Use these savings to your advantage and plan your meals around seasonal produce for the best value. See the chart in the appendix to determine when you should expect to find a fruit or vegetable at a bargain price based on its natural growing season.

TIP: Marked-down produce is not spoiled produce. In most cases it just needs to be used within a day or two of being purchased. Use this to your advantage and create a meal around the item or consider purchasing and freezing the item. We both pick up all of the marked-down bananas when we grocery shop to freeze for smoothies, and you can chop up peppers, onions, and more to freeze for soups and stir-fry meals.

Be sure you're storing your fresh produce properly to get the most bang for your buck:

- Did you know that tomatoes should not be refrigerated? That's right—keep them on your countertop.

- Herbs and greens do best in a moist environment, so wrap them in a damp paper towel and place them in a Ziploc bag when you get home from grocery shopping.

- Put peaches and other stone fruit in a brown paper bag to help them ripen more quickly, or move them to the fridge to slow down ripening.

- Store fruits and vegetables separately, as each can increase the ripening of the other. Products like the Blu-Apple (http://allingoodtime.net/bluapple) absorb ethylene gas and help extend the life of produce and cut down on waste as well.

- Winter squash, potatoes, and apples will keep for a long time in a cool, dark location such as a cellar. To make apples last longer, be sure to pull out any with bruises or soft spots before storing them.

- See more produce storage tips (and share your own!) at http://allingoodtime.net/produce.

Soda

Soda sales abound in the hot summer months, especially during the prime cookout weekends—Memorial Day, the Fourth of July, and Labor Day. You'll also find sales between Thanks-

Frugal Microwave Popcorn

Microwave popcorn can be an expensive treat, especially for large families, but you can easily make your own for a fraction of the cost.

Take a paper lunch sack and add one-third cup popcorn kernels. Tape the bag shut and microwave until there are several seconds between pops (the length varies between microwaves, so try it a couple times to get a feel for the right length for your microwave).

Transfer the popcorn to a bowl and drizzle with melted butter or sprinkle with salt, Parmesan cheese, or another seasoning.

---

giving and Christmas. However, soda is one of those items that you very rarely find a coupon on, and you're not likely to save more than about 30 percent off during a sale.

Snacks

Snacks go on sale pretty frequently at grocery stores, and coupons are pretty easy to come by, especially if it's a new product that the manufacturer wants consumers to try. What might surprise you, however, is that some of the best snack deals will pop up at drugstores, so be sure to scan those ads for bargains.

Ten Reasons You Shouldn't Plan a Weekly Menu

Although we believe menu planning can save you time, money and frustration, we wanted to share this tongue-in-cheek list of reasons why you might not want to menu-plan:

10. You're a nonconformist by nature, and since meal plans are popular, you refuse to give in.

9. You like to spend your free time staring blankly at the pantry trying to come up with dinner ideas. It's like a hobby.

8. You prefer the "seek and you shall find" method of mealtime. You stock the shelves and the fridge, and your family is required to seek-and-find their meals there.

7. You like to test your cooking skills by looking through the cabinets at 5:15 and creating a gourmet meal out of the random ingredients you find.

6. Your family enjoys having the same seven meals every week, so there's no need for a menu plan.

5. You're a free spirit and refuse to be bogged down with "organization" of any kind.

4. You want to be able to blame an empty refrigerator and pantry when you tell your extended family they can't drop by at dinnertime.

3. The grocery store is your "happy place" and you like making extra trips to pick up last-minute ingredients.

2. You want to do your part to boost the economy by spending lots of money at the grocery store, even if the food goes bad before you use it.

1. You like to use the excuse "We don't have anything to eat" as a reason to go out to dinner.

Mandi really likes Plan to Eat (http://allingoodtime.net/plan toeat), an online meal-planning service. Each week she plans her menu from her saved recipe book, and the service automatically creates her shopping list for her!

Alternative Ways to Source Produce

Aimée Wimbush-Bourque is an experienced professional chef who now runs the popular food blog SimpleBites.net. She shares these tips for sourcing quality produce outside of your local grocery store:

1. Garden. We've already talked about the value of a backyard garden in the first section. If you want to know exactly where your produce is coming from and what chemicals are used—or not used—your own backyard garden is your best source. Combine that with the price of harvest the fruits and veggies, and it's even better.
2. Community Garden. Community gardens allow a group of people to claim and tend to their own plots even if they don't have space in their yard.
3. Community-Supported Agriculture. Join a CSA to purchase directly from a farm near you. You'll be supporting

local farmers, and you'll have the opportunity to try lots of new fruits and veggies that you might not buy on your own.

4. Farmers' Markets & Roadside Stands. Farmers' markets and roadside stands are also great ways to support local farmers, and they give you more control over the selection and quantity of the produce you buy than a CSA.

5. Pick Your Own. Visit a U-pick farm for fresh fruit picked straight from the tree (or vine or bush). It's as fresh as it gets, and it's fun for the whole family.

Nursery/Kids' Rooms

BABY ANNOUNCEMENTS

Although custom photo cards and announcements can be expensive, you'll also find a lot of good deals on these if you watch for them (especially if your baby is born in late fall, so that you can take advantage of the deals that photo companies offer for Christmas).

BABY FOOD

There are often coupons and sales on baby food, and if you shop the sales cycles (which we talk about more in the grocery section), you can buy the baby food you need for less. But like most things, the least expensive way to feed your baby is to simply make the baby food yourself. While that sounds overwhelming, homemade baby food is actually really simple, especially for older babies who can handle some texture. Steam, boil, or bake a variety of fruits and veggies and then mash them up for inexpensive, nutrient-rich baby food. Our favorite book to help you get started is *Mommy Made and Daddy Too!* (http:// allingoodtime.net/mommymade), but Ruth Yaron's *Super Baby Food* (http://allingoodtime.net/superbabyfood) is another great choice. You can also find tons of information on the Internet at WholesomeBabyFood.com and NutureBaby.com.

BABY GEAR

Begin purchasing baby gear as soon as you're comfortable with the idea, usually sometime in your second trimester or at the beginning your third trimester. It will be easier to budget and watch for the best prices if you spread the purchases over several months rather than waiting until the end, but keep in mind that you may also receive a lot of what you need as shower gifts, especially with your first baby.

To save money, you can buy almost everything you need used or on consignment or, even better, borrow it from friends and family. Baby clothes and shoes are often passed down in great condition, and toys, playpens, high chairs, and maternity clothes don't wear out too quickly with little ones. However, it's important to always check for recalls before borrowing or purchasing an older model. The downside to borrowing baby gear and clothes is that the lender may ask for them back before you're really done with them, and then you'll be left needing to purchase replacements unexpectedly.

Allowance/Chores

The best time to start giving an allowance is when a child is old enough to understand that money is used to purchase things and that you actually have to work to receive it. There is some debate over whether to tie an allowance to a list of weekly chores to be performed or whether it's just a set amount each week, but the most important aspect in our opinion is to teach children how to budget. This is the perfect opportunity to demonstrate the importance of setting amounts for spending, saving, and charitable giving, as well as setting goals and attaining them. There are even cool piggy banks available that have separate compartments for each area of spending to help children actually see how their money is divvied up in different ways (http://allingoodtime.net/piggybank).

Mandi's family uses a hybrid method of chores and allowance that looks like this:

Each of their older girls has the opportunity to earn $3.50 a week (50 cents a day) through daily chores. They only receive payment if they do their jobs without being nagged, and there is no guarantee that they'll receive any of that money if they don't complete their chores. However, they also have chores that they're expected to do without payment each day simply because they are a member of the family.

In addition, Mandi regularly offers extra jobs to the first

taker. Jobs may include playing with the baby while she makes dinner, cleaning out the arts-and-crafts bin, dusting or straightening up after one of their younger sisters. There are not a ton of these opportunities, so the girls have to decide carefully each time if they want to take on the job or risk missing out on the opportunity to earn extra money until the following week.

There are lots of different methods for keeping track of chores as well, from marble jars to chore charts. We love the Melissa & Doug chore chart (http://allingoodtime.net/chore-chart), but if you're looking for a free printable chore chart to get started, we have a free one available here: http://allingoodtime .net/printablechorechart.

CHORES FOR KIDS
Daily and weekly chores help teach kids discipline and the importance of routines, which will help them when they're running their own households. That doesn't mean they need to spend hours a day on chores, but having a few small chores lays the foundation for a myriad of life lessons—from practical skills to responsibility and contributing to the family unit.

Two to three years old:
Two- and three-year-olds are especially eager to help with household chores, especially when you're by their side. Rather than asking them to pick up toys and then walking away, make cleanup fun by turning it into a game. Invite them to dust the lower shelves and furniture while you're dusting the higher places. And praise them for pitching in with a happy heart!

- Pick up toys.
- Put dirty clothes in hamper.
- Dust furniture.

Four to five years old:
Four- and five-year-olds are capable of a lot more than we often give them credit for. They are still eager to help but their skills have grown to match their eagerness.

- Make bed.
- Put clean laundry away.
- Wipe windowsills.
- Empty small trash cans.

Six to seven years old:
We've heard many mothers of older children say that everything gets easier when kids turn six or seven years old because they are suddenly able to really help in a way that makes a difference, and we've both found this to be true in our own families. That's not to say we never deal with bad attitudes when it comes to chores, but for the most part our six- and seven-year-olds are still willing helpers!

- Make lunch.
- Help fold clothes.
- Vacuum.
- Wipe bathroom sink.

Eight years old and older:
While eight-year-olds are certainly still kids and need plenty of time to play and just run free, they're also able to help out around the house at an age-appropriate level. Now is a great time to start teaching them to do laundry, cook simple dishes, take out the trash, and more!

- Do laundry.
- Help cook.
- Take out the trash.
- Clean the shower or tub.

BLANKIES & LOVIES

It's not uncommon for babies and toddlers to develop an attachment to a special blanket, stuffed animal, or other lovie, and several of our kids have their own special thing that they sleep with and cart around with them. We recommend buying a duplicate blanket or lovie when you start to see that extra-special attachment (since obviously you can't do it with every toy or stuffed animal your child loves) so that you have one available when the first one needs to be washed or gets lost or worn out.

What Baby Gear Do You Really Need?

With whole stores dedicated to baby gear, it can be hard to sort through what we actually need for our babies. Not surprisingly, there are a lot fewer things that you actually need than you'll find on the shelves in stores. Here is our list of baby necessities:

- car seat
- crib, co-sleeper, or Pack 'n Play
- stroller
- baby monitor
- a sling, wrap, or carrier

These items are optional and whether you'll need them will depend on your situation and your baby's temperament more than anything else:

- changing table/pad
- bath sling
- bouncy seat
- swing
- infant car seat (Mandi prefers to start her babies in a convertible car seat and just carry them in a sling when they're out and about)

And these are the items we don't think you really need at all:

- wipes warmer
- a quilt to match your nursery bedding set
- diaper genie
- baby tub

CAR SEATS

Unless you are borrowing from a very close friend or family member, you should always buy car seats new. Car seats only have a five-year shelf life and should *never* be used after even a minor traffic accident. Be sure to let your insurance provider know when car seats are involved in even a small fender bender. Tara's husband was rear-ended on his way to work several years ago, and even though none of their kids were in the car at the time, their insurance company cheerfully replaced all four car seats involved and took care of disposing of the old ones.

Although they're more expensive than their counterparts, we prefer Britax car seats, especially for infants, and the Graco Nautilus for older kids, which allows children to ride in a five-point harness until they're sixty-five pounds and converts easily to a high-back booster chair for children up to a hundred pounds. Not only do these models score extremely high in safety tests, but they're easier to install and use than some of their less expensive counterparts. However, the *best* seat for your family is one that fits both your car and your child well!

To keep your babies and children safe in the car, it's best to have a certified technician check your car-seat installation. You can find Child Seat Fitting Stations at SeatCheck.org, as well as tips for safe installation and use.

Be sure to check the laws in your state for car-seat use as well. In many states, children are required to ride in a booster until they're eight years old and eighty pounds. Although infants can be turned forward facing once they're twenty pounds and one year old, rear facing is actually much, much safer, and children can be kept rear facing until they're two to three years old.

Consumer Recalls

There are dozens of recalls each month on various household items and products, but baby gear and children's items are the most frequent. If you register your baby items when you buy them, you'll receive notices of any recalls. You can also sign up for email notifications or search current recalls at Recalls.gov. Not only is it important to keep track of recalls because of potential safety issues, but it's also illegal to sell, or even give away, recalled items. Often, all it takes is a quick fix with a kit from the company, but it's important that you check for recalls before selling any of your baby gear, clothing, or toys!

CLOTHING

The best time to buy kids' clothing is at the end of each season. Comb the racks to purchase ahead for the following year, adjusting for your children's growth. It's not always a perfect science and sometimes you'll estimate too big and sometimes too small, but even a few misses is okay when you're buying clothes at 50 to 70 percent off retail. The best time to buy basics like jeans is in October when retailers are discounting their overstock after back-to-school shopping.

Thrift stores are a gold mine, especially for kids' clothing. Tara bought a pair of Ralph Lauren jeans and two pairs of Old Navy jeans for her oldest son several years ago for $2.50. They've since been worn by her two younger sons and donated back to the thrift store in relatively the same condition as when she purchased them! Like adult clothing, you'll need to be prepared to really dig to find the best deals, and you'll find the best deals by visiting your local thrift store regularly. Go on their discount days to score even better deals.

TIP: The mystery of lost socks is one that we may never solve, but baby socks are even harder to keep track of than their larger counterparts. Mandi actually had a washing machine get completely backed up because of a tiny baby sock that was sucked down the drain! To prevent missing socks, wash them in a mesh lingerie bag. Save yourself some time by handing the whole bag over to your older kids to match the pairs for you.

Swimwear

Swimsuit sales start in July, with the lowest prices appearing in August and September. However kids' swimwear gets picked over much earlier than adult swimwear, so it's best to buy it sooner rather than later.

Selling Children's Clothing

Older clothes can be passed down to friends and family or donated, and there's a good market for gently used brand-name baby and toddler clothing in consignment shops and on eBay. If all else fails, there's always garage sales, but generally you'll get higher prices on eBay. The key to successfully reselling children's clothing is to buy brand-name clothes, since items from Walmart and other discount retailers don't hold their value. Many people even buy at consignment shops or on eBay and then resell the items the same way once they're done with them.

TIP: As we've added more children to our families, rotating their seasonal clothing has become a bigger and bigger chore. A couple of years ago, Mandi was so frustrated by the process of trying to figure out which clothes fit whom that she dumped out more than six large bins of clothing and started from scratch. She decided that each child would wear the clothes in only one size, even if it meant that some of the outfits were too big to wear at the start of the season and that there were other cute outfits packed away in different sizes that might still fit. When it's time to switch the clothes again, she simply packs each size into the appropriate box, pulling out the next season or size to replace it. To deal with sizing variances, she changes the size on the label of any clothes that don't fit according to their labeling.

DIAPERS

First-time parents are often shocked at the cost of diapering a child with disposable diapers. Experts estimate that the cost hovers somewhere around $1,500, and that's not even including disposable training and overnight pants! We're no strangers to the monthly pinch this can cause, especially since Tara had three children in diapers at the same time!

Here are a few tips on saving some cash on this basic necessity:

- Diaper coupons abound, so there's really no reason to purchase a package at full price. Be sure to sign up on all of the major brands' websites to receive some especially high-value coupons by mail. Encourage family members to sign up as well and pass them along.

- Toss brand loyalty out the window. This is definitely one area where you'll save the most by purchasing a variety of brands depending on what coupons and sales are available in a given week. And don't be afraid of store-brand diapers. They've improved by leaps and bounds over the past few years and many rival the quality of brand names at a significant savings.

- Watch the sales and gift-card offers like a hawk. Pairing a coupon with a good sale is the best way to save on any purchase, and the best way to save if you do have a preferred brand is to buy several packages when you come across one of these offers.

- Shop the online diaper sales at Amazon (http://allingood time.net/diapers) and buy extras when they hit rock-bottom prices.

- Consider starting a stockpile of diapers as soon as you find out you're pregnant. Here are some recommendations on how many of each size of diapers to purchase from BabyCheapskate.com:

Size N: Newborn diapers typically go up to ten pounds. At this age, you'll be changing baby's diaper often, so buy about a month's worth. (six to seven jumbo packs)

Size 1: Size 1 diapers typically fit babies between eight and fourteen pounds. Most babies will reach this weight at about three-and-a-half months. (fifteen-plus jumbo packs)

Size 2: Size 2 diapers typically fit babies between twelve and eighteen pounds. Most babies will reach this weight at about seven months. (twenty-five-plus jumbo packs)

Size 3: Size 3 diapers typically fit babies between sixteen and twenty-eight pounds. Babies often spend the longest in this stage, which can last up to two years old. (seventy-plus jumbo packs)

Size 4: Size 4 diapers typically fit babies between twenty-two and thirty-seven pounds, and for many kids this is the last size you'll need before they're potty-trained. (forty-plus jumbo packs)

These estimates are, of course, going to vary some based on the size of your baby at birth and how quickly he or she grows. All of Tara's babies except for one were in the eight-to-nine-pound range, so she barely used two jumbo packages of newborn diapers. Be sure to hold on to all of your receipts so you can exchange them for another size if necessary.

Our "stock-up price" for diapers is 22 cents per size 3 diaper (slightly more or less for bigger or smaller diapers) and 2 cents per wipe.

Cloth diapering is growing in popularity once again as an alternative to disposables. However, if you're looking to cloth-diaper purely to save money, be aware that most of the savings are negated by the additional time and money spent on laundering them. That's not to say that they don't have any benefits.

They're obviously better for the environment and may encourage toddlers to potty-train earlier. If you're interested in learning more, you can find a thorough guide to cloth diapering from Tsh at Simple Mom (http://allingoodtime.net/clothdiapers).

DIAPER BAGS

If you give birth in a hospital, you probably won't even need to purchase a diaper bag because you'll receive a complimentary formula gift bag as a patient. However, investing in a quality diaper bag that you love and that will last you for several years isn't a bad thing. Mandi received a Ju-Ju-Be diaper bag before the birth of her third daughter, and she used it for three years before passing it on to a friend in almost new condition!

Diaper bags come in a wide range of styles these days, so consider your needs carefully before purchasing. If you want your significant other to help with the carrying, you might consider purchasing a more gender-neutral bag. Deals abound online; just take a minute to do a quick Google search for discount and free shipping codes before you check out.

To be sure you have everything you need when you leave the house, restock your diaper bag each time you come home. You don't need to take a ton of stuff with you, and when we had babies, we mostly left our diaper bags in the car rather than hauling them around with us everywhere, but you will want to be sure you have plenty of diapers as well as a couple outfits and bottles for babies. It's always a good idea to keep an extra burp cloth or two on hand as well as an extra blanket for nursing. For toddlers, you'll want to have a sippy cup and small snack, like Gerber Puffs, as well as snacks for older children. We also like to keep a zippered pouch with small items like infant nail clippers, diaper-rash-cream samples, and a cocoa-butter stick for chapped faces and other dry patches. You could stick a lip gloss or feminine-care products in this pouch for yourself as well.

FORMULA

While breast-feeding is obviously the least expensive option—and we've found that it can be a lot more convenient too since there are no bottles to prepare—there are plenty of families who either choose or are forced to use formula. The costs of formula can quickly add up, but there are ways to minimize the expense!

Although there's not a "best time" to purchase formula, you will find that the prices at big-box stores are typically lower than grocery stores and drugstores. You'll save even more at a warehouse club when you buy in bulk. With the introduction of Amazon Mom (http://allingoodtime.net/amazonmom), you can also save by purchasing formula online at Amazon.com.

If you qualify for WIC in your state, there's no shame in taking advantage of the program. If you use formula, you'll receive vouchers toward your formula purchases, and if you breast-feed exclusively, you'll receive extra vouchers for things like eggs, milk, and other healthy staples. Tara's family used WIC for several years, and she wholeheartedly recommends it to new or expecting moms.

Rather than purchasing liquid formula, stick with the powdered formula. Although you'll lose out on some convenience, you'll save a significant amount of money. Likewise, unless your baby is on a special formulation for medical issues, try store brands rather than name-brand formula. If you need or prefer the name-brand stuff, be sure to get on the mailing list for your preferred brand because you'll receive coupons and other offers fairly regularly.

FURNITURE

Garage sales and consignment shops are great choices for picking up gently used kids' furniture. While we don't recommend purchasing used cribs unless you know the seller well, it's relatively safe to purchase other items used. Check to make sure that they're "true" and don't wobble, and avoid older items with peeling paint. Beyond structural issues, though, keep an open mind—a can of spray paint can make slightly battered items look like new.

HOMESCHOOLING

Mandi and her husband are just at the beginning of their homeschool journey, but Mandi was homeschooled during her senior year in high school, so they have some idea of what they're getting into. One misconception about homeschooling is that it costs a lot of money. Curriculum can cost a pretty penny, especially if you want to be able to use it straight out of the box without a lot of additional planning, but Jamie Martin of SimpleHomeschool.net and *Steady Days* (http://allingood time.net/steadydays) shares these tips for reducing your expenses:

The number one way to save on curriculum costs is by taking advantage of your library and interlibrary loans. With literature-based curricula like Sonlight, Ambleside Online, Five in a Row, and others, it's not always critical that you read the books exactly in the order presented by the teacher's guide, which lends itself well to the use of the library. Your library may also offer free passes for museums and other family activities that would make great field trips.

As a recovering perfectionist herself, Mandi understands the desire to have "brand-new" curriculum all too well, but borrowing, trading, and buying used is a great way to reduce your curriculum costs. If you belong to a co-op or homeschool group, organize a curriculum swap at the end of each year. Jamie's family has gotten free books and other supplies through these swaps. You'll also find used curriculum for sale at Homeschool Classifieds.com and on eBay, and the Home School Legal Defense Association (HSLDA) has a special curriculum marketplace for members as well. You can also sell your curriculum when you're done with it to offset the cost of new curriculum.

Finally, spread the cost of your curriculum across the entire year by creating a sinking fund for your curriculum needs. Jamie's family sets aside $20 per month per child, which doesn't make a huge dent in their monthly budget but makes it much easier to purchase supplies and curricula as needed. Homeschooling is radically affordable when compared with even the cheapest of private school options out there, and the cost per child goes down dramatically if you're able to use some of your materials with multiple children over time.

There are several popular planners and record-keeping programs available for homeschoolers. Donna Young's free homeschool planner (http://allingoodtime.net/donnayoung) is a popular choice, as is the Homeschool Tracker software (http://allingoodtime.net/homeschooltracker), which offers both a free and premium version. Mandi uses a BusyBodyBook planner (http://allingoodtime.net/busybodybook) for both planning and record keeping since she can plan each of her girls' assignments in its own column and make notes about books and supplies on the opposite page.

POTTY TRAINING

You'll hear a wide variety of advice on potty training depending on where you look. There's no right or wrong answer here, and if you do it differently than us, we don't mind! After nine children, though, we've decided that the best time to potty-train is when the child demands it. Although girls typically potty-train earlier than boys, Mandi's two middle girls each potty-trained at three years old with just a few accidents during the first couple of days. Tara's oldest daughter actually helped potty-train her little brother when he was two and a half, but Tara never forced the issue, just followed his lead.

Mandi's family prefers training potties because they're low to the ground and eliminate any fear or worry about falling into the potty, which can be an added stressor as kids are first learning. It hasn't taken long for her girls to start using the potty as a stepstool that they can use to sit on the big potty themselves, though. Mandi started keeping a small potty in the car after having to stop at a gas station by herself with a three-year-old, eighteen-month-old, and newborn for an emergency potty break.

Tara's family tried a potty chair with their oldest son but found that they were constantly cleaning up messes, and they've just used the regular toilet seat since then. Recently, however, Tara's husband replaced all of their toilet seats with a new model that has a smaller seat built in. It's magnetic, so it stays attached to the lid unless you pull it down for use, and the seat costs only about $5 more than a regular one.

SCHOOL SUPPLIES

The best time to buy school supplies is in August when they're marked as loss leaders at all of the major drugstores, office supply stores, and big-box stores. If you're willing to invest some time, you can pick up almost everything you need for a fraction of the cost by purchasing the items that are marked at ridiculously low prices each week and waiting on the rest. Remember to pick up extras of the things you know you'll use all year long, like crayons and glue sticks, since the prices are so much lower in August than at any other time of the year.

While Mandi has more flexibility in the school supplies she purchases as a homeschool mom, Tara is familiar with the de-

Displaying Kids' Artwork

Our kids go through piles of paper and craft supplies each week, creating this and making that, which inevitably leaves us with a growing pile of arts and crafts! Here are some of our strategies for dealing with artwork:

- Give each child a frame to display their artwork, changing it out regularly to showcase new pieces. Dynamic Frames are great frames that offer storage area in the back and make it easy to change the artwork regularly.
- Use a large bulletin board or hooks like Command's damage-free adhesive hooks to display artwork on a wall in your home.
- Hang a clothesline or ribbon and use clothespins to hang artwork from the line.
- Keep a file or box for each child to save extra-special pieces.
- Take pictures or scan the original artwork that you're not planning to save so that you'll still have a copy without having to store the hard copy.
- Mail artwork to relatives or friends with a special note.
- Don't be afraid to toss what's left. If your kids are like ours, there's too much to store all of it, and it's okay to throw some of it away!

tailed school supply lists that most schools send out these days. Rather than shopping exactly by this list, she picks up the loss leaders whenever it makes sense and donates what they don't need. She also takes the time to combine all of the kids' school supply lists in one master list that she can shop from rather than trying to juggle multiple lists.

SHOES

The best time to buy children's shoes is in July and August as stores try to move old merchandise to make room for the new back-to-school styles. We typically pass down only infant and toddler shoes because our preschoolers and older children are much too hard on their shoes to really pass them down, with the exception of dressy ones that are only worn occasionally.

Shoes are the hardest item to buy ahead of time because children's feet grow in spurts. However, if you have several small children, you can usually make your best guess, and even if you're wrong, someone will be able to wear them at some point!

TEACHING A CHILD TO RIDE A BIKE

The best time to teach a child to ride a bike is when they have the balance and coordination to do so, which doesn't necessarily come at a certain age. Motivation and confidence play a role too, and pushing your child to learn too soon can backfire. At age six, Tara had no interest in learning to ride until a friend who was a year younger came over and hopped on her bike, riding it up and down the street. Not wanting to be left behind, she learned how to ride it that very same day!

Jessica Fisher from LifeAsMom.com has a different approach from many. She and her husband teach their children by taking the pedals off their bikes so that they can first learn to balance without worrying about pedaling. Once they have this skill mastered (usually within ten or fifteen minutes), learning to pedal is a cinch!

TOYS

Postholiday clearance sales are perfect for stocking a gift closet, as well as purchasing ahead for next Christmas. Target is famous for their after-Christmas clearance with prices as low as 75 percent or more off retail in mid-January.

A Help-Wanted Bulletin Board

One idea we've seen that teaches kids the value of hard work is a help-wanted bulletin board. Basically, you post available jobs with a description and a rate, and kids can pick and choose the ones that they want to do. Creating a neutral place for these job ads gives children the opportunity to browse and choose the ones that appeal to them (and that they think are worth the money being offered in exchange for their time and effort), which is a fun way to practice negotiating, applying for jobs, and entrepreneurship, even for younger children.

To keep toy clutter to a minimum, Mandi's family practices the one-toy-in, one-toy-out rule. With a designated space for toys, they clean out their existing toys to make room for birthday and Christmas presents. Mandi always involves her kids in this process so that they don't feel like their toys are being given away behind their backs, but the space constraints of the toy cabinet make it easy to enforce.

To cut down on daily toy clutter, organize toys into sets—such as trains and train tracks, baby-doll accessories, LEGOs, building blocks, or kitchen sets. Toy sets enhance play, make cleanup easier, and promote sharing. They're also much easier to organize than individual toys. Rotate these toy sets—packing some away and switching them out every few months—to cut down on the mess and encourage your kids to play more with the toys that are available.

TIP: To make it easier for kids to clean up toys on their own, label bins and boxes with words (for readers) or pictures (for prereaders). Tara's family also found that bolting their toy bins

Homemade LEGO Table

When Tara's older boys outgrew their train table, she planned to donate it and purchase a LEGO table for them instead, but all of the ones she found online were very small and superexpensive. She and her husband purchased several square LEGO base pieces and screwed them right onto the existing train table, creating the perfect place for their kids to spread their LEGOs out and build their creations. (http://allingoodtime.net/legotable)

to the shelves rather than leaving them loose cut down on the dumping.

Garage sales are the best place to unload gently used toys. You may find that listing some sets that are complete and in exceptional condition will garner you higher prices on eBay, but unless an item is very rare, you're not going to get anything close to retail. In most cases we both opt to donate the toys we declutter or that our kids outgrow to help provide for less fortunate children.

Lice Prevention & Treatment

Neither of us thought much about lice until the day Tara and Luke took their kids in for a haircut and discovered that not one, not two, not even three, but all five of them had head lice. Head lice are quite prevalent among younger school-aged children, but Tara and Luke thought they were safe since their kids shower and bathe regularly. So imagine their surprise when they learned that it's actually easier for lice to attach to clean hair!

They later determined that one of the kids picked the lice up at school and it quickly spread to the others because they're often playing very closely and share beds from time to time. Now they're much more diligent about prevention, and they check the kids regularly for any signs of nits.

If you've never seen a nit, we'd encourage you to look at some photos online. They're slightly smaller than a sesame seed and are usually attached to an individual hair close to the scalp. The color ranges from clear to dark brown as the egg nears time to hatch, and it's easiest to see them in bright light.

Some tips Tara learned along the way:

- While we'd love to say that the all-natural removal methods Tara tried at first did the trick, ultimately she had to resort to one of the kits that contain pesticides to rid their family of these pests. She and her husband followed the instructions to a tee and rinsed thoroughly afterward.
- The plastic combs that come with the kits are worthless for actually removing anything. Look for the combs with metal teeth that are specially designed for removing nits.
- Removing the nits is essential after any kind of treatment. This is very time-consuming, so plan to spend as long as two hours on it depending on the length of your child's hair. Tara sat her oldest daughter down in front of their sliding-glass door and put on a movie to keep her occupied.

PREVENTING LICE:
- Teach your children not to share hats, scarves, hair ties, sports helmets, etc.
- Give each child their own personal combs, hairbrushes, and towels to use.
- Avoid head-to-head contact with other children.

Rec Room

AIRLINE TICKETS

According to FareCompare.com, the best time to purchase airline tickets is on Tuesday afternoons. Be sure to watch for sales and specials, because airlines often run special promotions. Tara and her family saved over $750 on flights to Florida for their family by holding out for one of Southwest's low airfare sales. As an added bonus, Southwest doesn't charge baggage fees and allows each passenger to check two bags, which are things you should consider—along with taxes and other fees—when calculating the total cost of a flight. Be sure to search for promo codes before booking a flight by typing the name of the airline plus promo code, e.g., Southwest promo code.

According to *ShopSmart* magazine, the best days of the week to fly are Tuesday, Wednesday, and Saturday. The cheapest time of day to fly is the red-eye, and when Mandi and her husband lived in Utah for two years, they often flew from Las Vegas to D.C. and back in the middle of the night for deep discounts. However, the trade-off is that you're exhausted, so it may not be worth the savings. You can also save by flying early in the morning and after lunch.

When flying, always be sure to check the TSA (Transportation Security Administration) website for any updated carry-on restrictions so that you don't end up having to throw something away at the airport. Arrive at the airport ninety minutes before your flight to give yourself plenty of time to get your baggage checked and through security. Most of the time you can check in for your flight at home and print your boarding pass, which significantly reduces the amount of time you'll have to stand in line. Also, if you have a smartphone, you may be able to go totally paperless and check in and display your boarding pass via an app!

BATTERIES

Look for deals on batteries in November and December when stores discount them for all of those holiday toy purchases. You can also frequently find batteries in the dollar section of many stores, and you'll often find printable coupons for these brands that can make the batteries very inexpensive or even free. If you live in a very warm climate, you might consider storing your batteries in a refrigerator to prolong their life. Just be sure to bring them back to room temperature before using them.

CONCERT TICKETS

To score concert tickets for less, check discount sites like Kayak.com or ScoreBig.com for bargain prices. It's also a good idea to register for your favorite artists' fan clubs since they often offer discounts or advance pricing to fans.

DVDS & BLU-RAY

It usually makes sense to rent movies for yourself unless you have a favorite movie that you plan to watch often. For kids, though, it's often more economical to buy them since children tend to watch their favorites over and over. You'll generally find the best pricing the week movies are first released on DVD or Blu-ray, and you can almost always find a printable coupon online to save even more on kids' movies during that week, so do a quick online search for those as well.

Amazon Video on Demand (http://allingoodtime.net/videoondemand) and Netflix (http://allingoodtime.net/netflix) both offer thousands of movies for instant streaming so that you can watch them from the comfort of your home without having to go to the store to get one or wait for them to arrive by mail. Redbox—the stand-alone movie rental kiosks that you find at many grocery stores, gas stations, and fast-food restaurants—regularly releases free one-night rental coupons, which Tara shares at Deal Seeking Mom (http://allingoodtime.net/redbox).

ELECTRONICS

You'll find the best deals on electronics between November and January. Companies will often offer gift cards or accessories with purchases that could yield a larger discount than a simple sale price. You may also find discounted pricing when new models are released in late spring and early summer. Electronics are often used as door busters during Black Friday sales events, and you can pick them up at deep discounts if you're willing to brave the crowds. Mandi and her husband have purchased both a TV and a Blu-ray player at these sales.

You'll find extra sales on TVs leading up to Super Bowl Sunday as well. You can always ask a salesperson if they can offer you any additional discounts or throw in additional accessories, such as stands, cables, etc., at no charge. You may be surprised at just how much leeway they have in making a deal even at the large chain stores.

Extended Warranty

Most experts agree that the cost of extended warranties on consumer electronics is not worth the investment. Like computers, however, if you are considering an extended warranty, be sure to check third-party sites like SquareTrade.com rather than purchasing through the company or retail store. To make the most of the manufacturer's warranty that comes with most electronics, be sure to create a file in your filing cabinet where you keep receipts and warranty information. Clean out this file once a year to get rid of any that have expired so you can quickly find those that are still valid.

Surge protectors are an inexpensive way to protect your electronics from electrical surges caused by lightning or other sources. Always use surge protectors with expensive or sensitive electronics. As an added bonus, surge protectors make it easy to prevent vampire power usage—the small amount of power that is still consumed by electronics even when they're powered off.

TIP: Tangled electrical cords in your entertainment center or computer desk can be frustrating and messy looking. Use cable ties or a cable tube to contain the mess of excess wires. To keep track of which plug goes with which electronic, use old bread tags or printed labels (folded over like flags) to label each cord. To reduce the number of cords for smaller personal electronics, consider a recharging mat that recharges these devices without any cords. Mandi has a neat trick for "tying" electronic cords to keep them neat and organized as well. Watch her video at (http://allingoodtime.net/cords).

EXERCISE

Save money by exercising at home with DVDs, which are inexpensive and effective (as long as you use them), and we both really like Jillian Michaels's videos. New fitness games for video consoles are amazing, and Tara especially loves the Kinect for its accuracy and integrated technology. It's like having a personal trainer right in your own living room.

Gym Memberships

You'll find the best pricing on gym memberships in January. Check out various gyms and ask if they offer free trial passes before you purchase. Then you can compare the benefits and prices among all of your local gyms before making a decision. Try to negotiate a price down at one gym by mentioning the deal that you saw at another. Consider paying month to month until you're sure that you're going to stick with your plan and that you really like the gym.

Best Time to Work Out

Although there are pros and cons of working out at various times of day, the best time of day to exercise is really the time that works best for your body and schedule. For some people, this is in the morning before other commitments and distractions get in the way. For others, it may be at lunch or during the afternoon. And for still others, like Tara, it may be late in the evening (while watching the Food Network!). Consistency is the key, so try to find the time that works best for your schedule because you'll be most likely to keep at it if it's convenient.

Exercise Equipment

You'll find the best prices of the year on home exercise equipment in January when many people are resolving to lose weight in the New Year. You'll likely also find some savings in late April and May when consumers are in a hurry to lose weight before beach season.

Consider going the do-it-yourself route before shelling out

money on home exercise equipment, though. You can probably make do without a treadmill in all but the coldest months, and a quick Google search turns up dozens of tips for making your own yoga mat and bag, using cans and water bottles as free weights, and plans for building your own aerobics step.

FABRIC

Fabric stores often have a section of discounted or clearanced bolts of fabric, and the larger chains frequently offer percentage-off coupons that allow you to pick up a single item for 40 percent off or save 20 percent off your entire order. Most of them will allow you to use the coupons on the clearance fabric, helping you get high-quality fabrics at a steep discount.

Tara's mom used these coupons to put together a nice basic sewing kit for Tara as a gift. Stores frequently offer sewing notions at 50 percent off, so if you combine the sale items with the store coupons, you can save big.

TIP: Inexpensive fabrics are a great way to dress up your home. Tutorials abound online for easy homemade pillow coverings, DIY bulletin boards, and custom window treatments. They also make a fantastic reusable gift wrap, so keep a small stash on hand for when inspiration strikes.

FAIRS

Saving money at the county or state fair isn't so much about actually saving money as it is about setting a budget and expectations before you go. You can always pack some bottled water and snacks to cut back on food expenses, and often purchasing a ride bracelet will save you money if you plan to ride many rides (although Tara's family no longer rides the fair rides since the one time they let their kids ride the kiddie roller coaster, it actually broke down with all five kids on it in the middle of the track). Most importantly, set expectations as far as games and food before you arrive to avoid any tantrums and whining.

GOLF

Golf can be an expensive hobby, but there are plenty of ways to reduce your costs. Groupon and other daily deals sites often have discounted deals on local golf courses, so keep an eye out for those specials. Just be sure to read the terms carefully for any blackout dates or other issues.

If you plan to play frequently, consider purchasing a course membership. Similarly, if you prefer the driving range, check out prepaid range plans. Renting clubs can add up over time, but a full set of brand-new golf clubs isn't cheap. Unless you're competing in the PGA Tour, you should be okay with a lesser-known brand, and be sure to check Craigslist or garage sales for good used sets. Similarly, purchase lower-end balls or X-out balls, which are golf balls with small flaws that won't affect your game. Finally, skip the golf-cart rental and walk the course. Not only will you save money, but you'll get into shape too. You can also bring your own bottled water and snacks rather than buying from the clubhouse.

LUGGAGE

March, May, and July are prime times for finding discounts on luggage. Look for luggage that you can both pull on two wheels or roll on four wheels for added convenience. When flying, tie a bright ribbon or use a brightly colored luggage tag to make your suitcases stand out from the crowd.

To save space in your luggage, pack carefully rather than tossing everything in haphazardly. Space-saving bags (or even Ziploc bags) allow you to squeeze the air out as you pack and leave a lot more room in your bag. Tightly roll clothing to save space and reduce wrinkles. Be sure to use travel-size toiletries (or create your own with a set of plastic bottles, which you can pick up at the dollar store or in the travel section of many stores for a dollar).

When you reach your destination, refrain from just leaving your luggage on the floor. Use the luggage stands whenever possible, as this will deter any possible bedbugs from making the return trip with you.

Download or print our free packing lists at http://allin goodtime.net/packinglist.

MUSIC

We both really enjoy music, especially when exercising or cleaning, and these days there are so many ways to find music for less! Tara purchases most of her music on iTunes using gift cards she earns through Swag Bucks, and Mandi and her family really enjoy Pandora, which allows them to create custom radio stations featuring their favorite artists for just $30 a year. Amazon.com and iTunes both feature free singles every week as well, which is a fun way to expand your collection and discover new artists.

PARKS & MUSEUMS

Many state and national parks and museums offer family memberships and reciprocal programs that can save you significant money throughout the year. Mandi and her family are lucky enough to live close enough to D.C. to regularly visit the Smithsonian Institute museums and the National Zoo for free, but they also purchase an annual pass to their local children's museum, which gives them entry to more than 165 children's museums throughout the United States and Canada. Similarly, Tara and her family have an annual membership to the Columbus Zoo, which not only makes it more affordable to visit the zoo several times a year, but also allows them to visit other zoos when they travel.

The National Park Service offers a National Parks and Federal Recreational Lands Pass that gives you free entrance to more than four hundred national parks, and they've also been running free national park weekends several times a year for the past few years, when you can visit any national park for free during the promotion dates.

Family memberships to parks, museums, and other activities can be very economical for a larger family if you'll use it more than two or three times during the year. You'll often receive special benefits on top of the free or discounted admission for your family. Keep in mind that many museums are closed on Mondays, so check their schedule before planning a visit. When possible, head to museums early in the day or late in the afternoon to avoid the midday crowds.

Mandi's family has discovered that homeschoolers often have an advantage because they can visit places during the school year while everybody else is in school. There's always the chance of showing up on the same day as school groups, but you'll find fewer school groups at the very beginning and very end of the school year as well as right before and after school holidays, so try to plan your trips for those times.

PETS

The time and energy involved in caring for a pet is often much more than you anticipate, especially when you're caring for a young family as well. Before getting a new pet, consider the cost of food, medical care, and other items such as leashes, bedding, etc. You'll also want to think about what you'll do with your pet while traveling. For dogs, be sure to consider their energy level, how much exercise they need, what kind of fencing you'll need, etc. (Mandi and her husband had an Alaskan Klee Kai—a miniature husky—who could jump over the seven-foot stone wall in their backyard.) Be sure to research the temperament of any pet you're considering before purchasing or adopting it. Some breeds are high-strung and more likely to snap at children, and others may be hard to housebreak. Many dogs end up being turned over to the pound because they aren't a good fit for the family, and this can be avoided through proper research.

While you might be tempted to visit the pet store to purchase your pet, many of these animals come from puppy mills or disreputable breeders. Not only do you encourage and keep these breeders in business by purchasing from pet stores, but the animals tend to be less healthy and more prone to illness as well.

Find reputable breeders through the American Kennel Club at AKC.org or through a veterinarian or local breed clubs. Buying from reputable breeders will almost certainly cost more than purchasing from the pet store, so if you're not worried about purebred animals, be sure to check your local shelter regularly. With a little patience, you're likely to find a puppy or a well-trained older dog that's perfect for your family!

It may be best to wait until summer vacation to get a new pet when kids are home from school and can be involved in getting the pet acclimated and settled in their new home.

To save on medical costs for your pets, take advantage of free neutering and spaying services in your area. You can also ask if your clinic offers vaccination clinics or specials to cut costs. Remember that regular visits can preempt larger expenses down the road. And as with medical costs for yourself, ask if your veterinarian gives a discount for paying in cash.

RESTAURANTS

Many people will tell you that the way to save money on restaurants is to simply eat at home. While that's definitely true, we both enjoy eating out with our families. There are plenty of ways you can save on the costs of eating out to stretch your budget, though. The easiest ways to save money are to order water instead of soda and to skip the appetizers. The typical restaurant meal offers plenty of food, but if you feel like you need something more, opt for restaurants that offer free chips or peanuts so that you're not paying extra for an appetizer. The cost of kids' meals can quickly add up if you have several children, so rather than ordering off the kids' menu, order something off the adult menu and split it between two to three of your kids.

Many restaurants now offer rewards clubs that let you earn free meals and discounts when you use your card. Mandi's family loves T.G.I. Friday's, and their Give Me More Stripes club is one of the best out there, with free chips, extra coupons and bonus offers, and the opportunity to earn an $8 coupon for every $100 you spend.

Be sure to sign up for birthday offers at all of your favorite restaurants as well. Many restaurants offer free desserts or appetizers during your birthday month, and you'll also get a free drink of your choice at Starbucks! See the full list of birthday deals at Deal Seeking Mom (http://allingoodtime.net/birthdaydeals).

For local restaurants and smaller chains, be sure to check Restaurant.com for discounted gift cards. Twenty-five-dollar gift cards are regularly priced at $8, and they often discount these to $1 or $2. What's the catch? Many of these gift certificates require you to make a minimum purchase of $35 to $50, but if you have larger families like we do, you easily spend that much on a single meal, and you'll still be able to treat the whole family for as low as $11 plus tax and tip if you do it carefully! Mandi and her family like to have their girls' birthday parties at Ledo Pizza, and they can do a party for almost twenty people for just $75, including a very generous tip, with these certificates.

To save time when dining out, avoid the dinner rush on the weekends. This doesn't mean you can't go out to eat on the weekends, but it's generally better to go early or late to avoid the crowds and long waits. Some restaurants, like Olive Garden and Logan's Roadhouse, offer call-ahead seating. If your goal is to eat and leave quickly rather than linger, be sure to check the menu online before you go so that you can order right away. You can also ask for your check as soon as your food comes so that you can leave when you're finished rather than waiting to pay.

ROAD TRIPS

To save on gas while traveling by car, we recommend GasBuddy .com, which helps you find the least expensive gas stations and can also calculate the cost of a road trip and make recommendations on where to stop for gas along the way.

Although a road trip with young kids may sound stressful, it can be a lot of fun if you plan carefully. Many people like to leave in the evening so that their kids will sleep through the night, but Mandi and her husband (who regularly drive to North Carolina and Florida from West Virginia) prefer to leave in the wee hours of the morning. To prevent extra stops, plan on stopping every three-to-four hours and let everybody get out, stretch their legs, and use the bathroom. To prevent potty emergencies with younger children, Mandi always carries a small training potty in the car so that they can stop on the side of the road without hunting down a dirty gas-station bathroom.

Avoid driving on the major holidays—especially Thanksgiving, but also the Friday before Memorial Day and Labor Day—so that you don't waste time sitting in traffic. We also learned the hard way that you don't want to leave the Outer Banks in North Carolina on a Saturday morning to drive up the East Coast after it took both of our families more than twice the normal time to get home after our joint vacation! We'd imagine this is true for other popular vacation destinations too.

Save money when traveling by car by carrying a cooler with drinks, snacks, and sandwiches so that you don't have to stop at gas stations or fast-food restaurants. Avoid salty snacks, sugary drinks, and caffeinated drinks to cut down on the number of bathroom breaks you'll need to make.

Depending on the ages of your children, how you're traveling, and how long your trip will take, it's always a good idea to have activities ready to keep kids busy and engaged while on the road. Some of our favorites include:

- discovery bottles
- Mad Libs or other activity books
- magnets and a cookie sheet
- road-trip games
- stories on tape
- children's music
- books
- DVDs
- Magna Doodles

SHOPPING

Brick & Mortar Stores

Stores like Kohl's, Gymboree, and Crazy 8 regularly offer sales and store gift-card bonus events where you earn credits toward future purchases based on the amount that you spend. Most brick-and-mortar stores also have price guarantees so that if you buy something and it goes on sale within seven-to-ten business days, you can have your receipt adjusted and receive cash back. Old Navy has, perhaps, the best policies on this, and you can actually take your receipt in, have them scan it, and they'll automatically make those adjustments for you. You can also purchase their "one-day wonder" sale items ahead of time and then have the receipt adjusted on the day of the sale, which is a great way to take advantage of limited-quantity deals without having to wait outside the store at opening!

Daily Deal Sites

Daily deal sites such as Groupon and Living Social offer a wide variety of deals at deep discounts, often for just one day or a certain number of redemptions. For example, last year Living Social offered $20 Amazon.com gift cards for just $10. The downside to this type of shopping is that you can get caught up in the hype and purchase a voucher or coupon for something you don't really need. You also need to keep track of the expiration dates of the vouchers you do purchase to make sure they don't expire. On the other hand, it's a great way to get the things you purchase anyway (such as clothing from your favorite retailer) at a discounted price, and designer sites like Rue La La and Gilt make these luxuries much more affordable. We've put together a full list of our favorite daily deal sites at http://allingoodtime.net/dailydeals.

eBay

EBay is a great place to find hard-to-find used items as well as brand-new items at a fraction of the cost. The key is to keep your emotions separate from your bidding and to have a strategy going on.

The best time to bid to win is right as the auction is about to end. Bidding too early can drive up the price unnecessarily through bidding wars. Auctions that end early in the morning on a Monday or Tuesday generally have less traffic, so a great strategy is to specifically target auctions that end during those times. And of course, you can always employ an auction sniping service to do your dirty work and place a bid on your behalf at the last possible second.

Tara and her husband have had a lot of success selling some of their older collections—such as *Star Wars*, Transformers, and Fiestaware—on eBay, as well as their Camaro Z28. In their experience, it pays (literally) when you're listing auctions to time them to end during a high traffic time period. More traffic equals more bids, especially since most bids are placed during the closing minutes of auctions. The optimal time to end an auction is on Sunday evenings between 8 P.M. ET and 10 P.M. PT.

Flea Markets

Don't be afraid to haggle when shopping at flea markets. Most sellers mark their prices up by at least 10 percent to allow for customers to ask for discounts. Ask if the seller gives discounts for paying with cash or offer to pay one discounted price for a bundle of several items since sellers really don't want to haul all of their merchandise back home again. Carry your own bottled water and snacks to avoid paying premium prices for "fair food."

Online

No matter what you're shopping for, never make an online purchase without first doing a quick Google search for promo codes or free shipping codes. The most effective search is to type the name of the store along with "promo codes," "coupons," or "free shipping codes."

Register with cash-back sites like Ebates or ShopAtHome (http://allingoodtime.net/cashback), and when you click through these sites to make a purchase, you'll receive a percentage of your purchase back at a later date.

When making a large purchase, be sure to search price comparison sites such as Google Product Search, PriceGrabber, or NexTag, each of which collects data from all over the Internet to show you where you can find the best deal.

Yard Sales

When shopping at garage sales, the key is to be patient and look for hidden treasures. Something might be a great deal, but if you don't need it or have an idea for how you'll use it, you probably shouldn't buy it (unless you know you can sell it for a profit and you'll actually follow through and do that). Although it's not always easy to do, be willing to negotiate with sellers. Most of them have probably priced their items a little higher than they actually hope to sell them for, and you should get the best price you can!

To see the best selection of items, arrive early on the first day of a sale. If you're planning on hitting several sales, map out your route ahead. Carry cash in small bills to give you more negotiating power. And if you're looking for the best deals, head back on the last day of the sale to get even better prices on the remaining merchandise.

Black Friday Shopping Tips

- Make a list.
- Prioritize by store and item.
- Be realistic about how much you'll get done.
- Take a shopping buddy.
- Leave the kids at home.
- Research prices ahead of time.
- Wear layers.
- Bring snacks and water.
- Be friendly.
- Carry the sale ads with you.
- Or . . . wait until Cyber Monday, when you'll find great deals online.

SKIING

Skiing can be a fun winter activity for the whole family, but the costs can also add up quickly. If you ski regularly, the costs of your own equipment and season passes are valuable investments and will likely save you money over the course of the season. For more casual skiers, see if you can borrow equipment from family or friends to avoid paying rental fees. Avoid the crowds and ski for less by skiing during the week rather than on the weekends. For a full ski vacation, book well in advance, as early as spring for the following winter, for the best pricing and availability.

TIP: For skis, snowboards, and other winter sports gear, be sure to call your local ski shop and ask about upcoming ski swaps.

SPORTING EVENTS

Although you may want to splurge on full-priced tickets to see your team play their rival team, you can enjoy sporting events for less by waiting for family nights, which offer four-packs of tickets plus food at a discounted price, or by going to minor league games instead of major league. Avoid the hefty prices of stadium food and drinks by eating beforehand or bringing your own. Just be sure to check the stadium rules since many won't allow you to bring in open containers for security reasons.

SUMMER ACTIVITIES

We both have fond memories of summer camps and other summer activities, but we know how quickly costs can add up, especially if you have several children! Many camps, however, offer early-bird rates, so plan early to take advantage of these. You may also be able to find sibling discounts for enrolling more than one child in the same camp program. If it's truly a hardship to pay for summer camp, you may be eligible for financial assistance or scholarships. Day camps also qualify for the child-care tax credits, so make sure you keep careful records of your costs.

Many churches and libraries also offer summer programs for free, and your city or county parks and recreation department may offer a variety of free and paid activities and lessons as well.

TIP: Because gas prices are the highest during summer travel months, look for opportunities to carpool with friends and neighbors to camps and other activities. You can trade off and enjoy some extra time to yourself as well!

Staycations

Staycations have become a popular alternative to the traditional vacation in recent years as families look for ways to save money while still carving out quality time together. But a staycation doesn't have to be boring! Plan ahead to make the most of your time off:

- Camp in the backyard.
- Visit the local tourist traps that you usually avoid.
- Plan theme nights, such as movie-and-popcorn night, homemade pizza night, family game night.
- Head to the park for a picnic and afternoon of playing.
- Spend the day at a local pool or water hole.
- Have a camp day and invite your kids' friends over for games and activities.
- Go hiking or biking on a local trail.

- Go to a baseball game.
- Visit a local zoo or museum.
- Organize a block party for the neighbors.
- Go see a movie.
- Plan a craft day.
- Visit the library.

VACATIONS

If your goal is to save money, vacationing during the off-seasons is always going to be the least expensive option. In most cases, the most expensive parts of vacation are the transportation and lodging. Rather than staying in a hotel, look for time-share rentals or—if you're brave enough—consider a home swap. Sites like HomesforSwap.com actually connect individuals and families who are interested in swapping homes for a vacation, and you'll save on the cost of lodging and often the cost of renting a car as well.

Be sure to book your lodging well in advance, especially for popular vacation destinations. Book your hotel room not only for your final destination but for any stops you'll make along the way as well. Tara and her entire family ended up spending the night in their SUV in a Walmart parking lot one year because they assumed that they'd be able to find a hotel along the way—and that's not a pleasant way to start a vacation.

When we travel with our families, we look for places that include a kitchen or kitchenette. Eating out for every meal can get expensive, so plan to eat most of your breakfasts and lunches in to save money. Tara and her family always stock up on water, quick breakfast items, and staples such as bread, peanut butter, and jelly ahead of time. When eating out, look for restaurants that offer Kids Eat Free (http://allingoodtime .net/kidseatfree) specials to reduce the cost of your meals.

Talk to locals, who are often the best source for finding fun things to do and places to eat that are off the beaten path and less crowded. Your hotel concierge will also have recommendations and ideas that you may not have thought of. Mandi's husband loves to browse the pamphlets that you find in hotel lobbies and other tourist traps. These are great for discovering fun activities and often offer coupons and discounts as well. In the months leading up to your trip, check social shopping sites regularly for your destination to see what activities and deals pop up in that area.

Beach

Although each area has its own attractions and specialties, you'll always save money by staying across the street from the ocean rather than in an oceanfront property. Move a couple more blocks inland to save even more. Prices drop dramatically after Labor Day, so a late summer vacation may be the way to go if you have that flexibility.

Cruises

To save money on cruises, book well in advance *or* at the last minute if you have that flexibility. Packages that include airfare aren't generally any cheaper than purchasing your plane tickets directly, so skip those and watch for better deals on your own. Many cruise lines offer a complimentary lunch to those boarding the ship on the day that it sets sail, so plan on arriving early and take advantage of a free meal while others are still checking in.

While meals are included in your cruise package, usually the only beverages included are tea, water, and juice. Purchase a soda card your first day on board to limit your costs to about $4 per day. Pack carefully because those little incidentals that you forget at home (like toothbrushes and toothpaste) cost a pretty penny once you've set sail. The excursions arranged by the cruise lines can be expensive, and you can save money by walking a block or two away from the dock and making your own arrangements.

Disney World/Disneyland

Disney World may be the happiest place on earth, but that happiness comes with a hefty price tag. That said, we both love Disney World and have recently done full-week trips with our families. There's no way to really *do* Disney without spending money, but there are definitely ways to save while you're there. Don't be afraid to splurge a little, but look for ways to save on the areas that matter less so that you can spend a little more in the areas that matter more!

The biggest expense is going to be your park tickets. Remember that the price per day drops significantly while you're there, so a four-day ticket costs just a few dollars more than a three-day ticket and so on. To stretch your budget, stay off-site at a non-Disney hotel or in a rented villa, since these are much less expensive than the Disney resorts themselves. You can take your own food into the parks, so a hotel room with a kitchenette is the perfect solution if you're willing to prepare a picnic lunch and snacks to take with you (renting a locker for your stuff is much less expensive than buying food in the parks!). Similarly, pack refillable bottles and stick with water to save on drink expenses. Tara's family takes powdered drink-mix packets to entice their kids to drink more!

TIP: You'll also save money by buying souvenirs ahead of time rather than in the park. Even better, buy a collection of Disney Trading Pins before you go and spend your trip swapping pins with the characters at the park in lieu of souvenirs. If you'll be at the park in the evenings, you definitely want to take some glow necklaces and bracelets with you so that you don't have to buy them in the park. Dollar stores and the Target dollar spot are great places to stock up on these for cheap. An inexpensive autograph book also makes a great souvenir!

Although Mandi and her family have been to Disney in the heat of summer before, the best time to go is in the spring or fall. Not only is there milder weather, but the parks are much less crowded, so you'll be able to ride more rides and generally enjoy yourself more. No matter what time of year you go, look for rides with the Fastpass option, which allows you to claim a place in line without actually standing in line the whole time!

Disney Planning Resources

Although we both love Disney, we're hardly experts. The key to making the most of your Disney vacation is really in planning ahead of time. Here are some great resources to get you started:

- The Unofficial Guide Walt Disney World 2011 (http://allin goodtime.net/unofficialguide)
- TourGuideMike.com
- MouseSavers.com
- AllEars.net
- The MouseforLess.com
- WDWInfo.com

Grand Canyon

The Grand Canyon is a beautiful, awe-inspiring place to visit, and there are a lot of different activities available—from flying over the Canyon in a Cessna to riding donkeys down into it. Whether you're that daring or just want to stick with a basic hike around the edge, you can save money by staying in a nearby city rather than right at the Canyon or by camping instead of staying in a hotel. The North Rim of the Canyon is much less crowded than the South Rim, and when they lived in Utah, Mandi and her husband actually drove out to an area that was so far off the beaten path that they didn't see another single person. (Of course, they also got lost without any idea of where they were and no cell signal, so maybe that's not the best way to go.) You'll find free attractions in the touristy areas as well, such as the Tusayan Museum and Ruin and the Desert View Watchtower.

New York City

Vacations to New York City are always going to come with a high price tag, but you can cut your costs considerably by traveling in January through April when the hotels are relatively empty after the holiday season. Of course, the trade-off is that you're likely to experience some bitter weather, but shoppers should be able to snag some decent bargains if they're willing to brave it.

Early spring is another good choice. Hotel prices start creeping up, but the weather will be considerably nicer, allowing you to walk to many of your destinations so that you can save on transportation costs. Plus, a walking tour of NYC is the ultimate frugal vacation entertainment. Can't-miss destinations include FAO Schwarz, Times Square, Grand Central station, and of course Central Park—all free!

The best way to save on Broadway tickets is to wait and purchase rush or standing-room tickets on the day of the performance. Since availability varies for each show, call the ticket office of the show you'd like to see for more information. You'll also find three TKTS booths around New York City where you can purchase same-day tickets for 25 to 50 percent off retail. Finally, sign up for the newsletters of any shows you really want to see because they often send out special sales and discounts.

Williamsburg, Virginia

Save money in Williamsburg, Virginia, by staying outside of the main Williamsburg area and driving in for your daily activities. There's lots to see in colonial Williamsburg even without an admission ticket (although a ticket will give you access to more buildings, activities, and exhibits), so if you're looking for a cheap way to tour the town, just park in one of the lots near Merchant Square and walk Duke of Gloucester Street.

Washington, D.C.

Washington, D.C., is full of free attractions, including the Smithsonian Museums, the Kennedy Center, and of course the other memorials throughout the city. You can also take a free tour of the Bureau of Engraving and Prints to see money being printed in real time, or print a self-guided walking tour from Cultural Tourism DC and spend the day exploring the city.

The good news is that flights into the D.C. area are typically among the least expensive since it's a major metropolitan area and you can choose between BWI, Dulles, and Reagan National. However, hotel accommodations are fairly expensive, so you may want to stay outside the city and rent a car if you plan to do a lot of driving anyway.

Yellowstone National Park

Touring Yellowstone National Park isn't superexpensive anyway since you can purchase a one-week pass for your vehicle, but if you're short on time and don't want to pay the fee, you can view the Grand Tetons from Route 89 or from U.S. 191 near Jackson, Wyoming.

VIDEO GAMES

Video-game manufacturers count on hard-core gamers to drive initial sales of new releases, but once the hype dies down after a few weeks, you'll find these still fairly new releases priced an average of $10 less than their initial offering price.

Purchasing gently used games at discounted prices at stores like Game Stop is also an option. The best part about buying used is that you are not only getting a great price, but the stores also guarantee that the games work, plus if you decide you don't like the game, you have seven days to exchange it for another used game. This is perfect for fickle kids who decide that a particular game isn't really what they wanted after all. Game rental services like GameFly can also be a good option if you don't want to invest a lot of money in the latest games.

Holiday & Event Planning

HOLIDAYS

The holidays *can* be stressful, but with a little planning, they don't have to be. Plan ahead rather than waiting until the last minute to minimize your stress and maximize the fun! Mandi has put together a series of free holiday ebooks and planners that you can download at http://allingoodtime.net/holidayebooks.

Christmas Cards

Purchase next year's Christmas cards ahead of time during Christmas clearance events in late December and early January. If you'd rather do a custom photo card, watch for deals in November and early December to get personalized cards for a steal. Often you can get free address labels around this time too, so all you'll pay is the cost of shipping your cards to you plus postage to your recipients.

Print your labels early in the season so that they're ready and waiting. Similarly, if you do a newsletter, you can write it well ahead of time, before the busyness creeps in, so that you don't have that hanging over your head.

Halloween

There are a number of ways to save on Halloween costumes. The first is, of course, to make them yourself. Mandi always had homemade costumes growing up, thanks to her crafty dad, which included everything from Cousin It to a spider. One year her brother even went as the Energizer Bunny, which allowed him the added bonus of being able to visit each house twice ("Still going..."). You can also save by reusing or passing down costumes within your family or swapping costumes with other families. Or stock the dress-up closet with costumes you purchase on clearance after Halloween and choose from those the next time the holiday rolls around.

Grocery stores and drugstores offer tons of sales on Halloween candy in October, and manufacturers typically put out a fair number of coupons as well. Combine the sales and coupons for great deals, and stock up after Halloween for other parties and holidays.

Holiday Decor

Shop holiday clearance events after each holiday for discount decor to use the following year. Check garage sales and thrift stores for discount seasonal decor as well.

Holiday Meals

Grocery stores know the typical components of holiday meals and will discount these products in the weeks leading up to the holiday. Be sure to check your Sunday paper, because manufacturers will often release high-value coupons for these items to encourage consumers to purchase their brand rather than a competitor's product. Many grocery chains offer free turkey or free ham incentives in the weeks leading up to a holiday, so pay attention to these and adjust your shopping needs as necessary to meet the minimum spend amounts required.

Whatever you do, don't wait until the last minute. Not only will you miss out on the best deals earlier in the season, but the stock is likely to be picked over and possibly depleted, and you'll have to combat other harried last-minute shoppers every step of the way.

To minimize the stress of preparing a holiday meal, start by writing down all of the dishes that you plan to prepare. Think about which of them can be prepared ahead of time and either frozen for a couple weeks or stored in the refrigerator for a couple of days. Then write out a time line, working backward from the time you want to serve dinner and scheduling things to be ready at a certain time. For instance, rolls are usually best served straight out of the oven, so schedule those to go in—and come out—last. On the other hand, you can keep stuffing (or dressing, depending on what part of the country you're from) and mashed potatoes warm on a hot plate, so you can prepare those a little earlier. Likewise, the turkey needs to rest once it comes out of the oven, so you'll want to figure out what time it should come out and then count backward to figure out what time it should go in.

TIP: Tara likes to purchase the aluminum-foil trays from warehouse clubs to cook holiday meals. They're the perfect size to prepare larger quantities and cleanup is a breeze. Plus you'll pay at least 50 percent less than if you purchase the same trays at your local grocery store.

Valentine's Day

Children's Valentine's Day parties don't have to be expensive. Many stores offer very inexpensive packages of valentines in the weeks leading up to the holiday, but you can also find numerous free printable valentines online. Just Google "free Valentine's Day cards."

You'll also find Valentine's Day candy on sale in the weeks before the holiday. Pair these sales with a coupon to save even more.

Roses are the primary choice for Valentine's Day, which is why you'll pay a premium price for them during this time. Consider choosing another flower to keep some extra cash in your wallet.

However, our very best tip for saving on Valentine's Day is to just wait to celebrate the day after. Not only will you save a bundle on flowers and candy, but you'll also avoid the long waits at dinner or the movie theater!

PARTIES

The best time to have a party is when the people you invite can come! We know that's a little oversimplified, but there aren't too many hard-and-fast rules here. In general, Saturdays are easier for the majority since most people don't have work or church. Schedules are usually much busier in June (for graduations and weddings) and December (for obvious reasons), so avoid those months if possible. According to GoodCooking.com, people prefer parties that start earlier in the winter and later in the summer.

Cakes

The best way to save on cakes is to make your own, but if you're short on time, stick with the plain cakes in the bakery case and add your own characters or themed items to them rather than buying a themed cake. If you want to bake a cake on your own but aren't sure if you have the necessary skills, cupcakes are a great way to practice. Because cupcakes are trendy these days, you don't even have to reveal that you did it because you were unsure!

Cake pops (http://allingoodtime.net/cakepops) are another trendy option, but keep in mind that there are additional up-front costs involved in purchasing sticks, edible pens, various sprinkles, and decorations, etc. If you plan to make them regularly, your expenses will be worth the investment because you can use various ingredients for multiple batches, but it may be fairly expensive if you're just doing it once.

Favors

Whether you're throwing a birthday party or a baby shower, save money on favors by shopping the dollar section at popular big-box stores or the dollar store itself. In general, it's best to avoid a lot of candy at birthday parties so the parents of your guests don't have to deal with it when the kids get home. Rather than sending home a bag of toys that will likely get lost or broken, Mandi usually does a craft with the kids at her girls' birthday parties, and the finished project is their favor. We've also heard of families who do a book swap in lieu of gifts.

Gifts

The best time to shop for gifts is all year long. Watch for sales and clearances on items that would make great gifts for the people you love and keep a gift closet so you can "shop" for gifts at home as needed. You'll find great deals right before the holidays as stores try to lure customers in and even better deals right after the holidays.

TIP: If you're purchasing a gift for a specific person, be sure to label it when you add it to your gift closet so that you don't forget in the interim and give it away to someone else!

Invitations

For birthdays, graduations, and showers, it's perfectly acceptable these days to send electronic invitations, or e-vites, as opposed to traditional invitations. Evites.com is the most popular service for doing this, but many people are also turning to Facebook or just sending regular emails for casual parties. If you have your heart set on traditional invitations, start at the dollar store for the least expensive ones. You can also create your own custom invitations through photo printing sites, and if you plan far enough in advance, you might even be able to do it for just the cost of shipping. With the rising cost of postage, you can still save money by handing them out in person rather than mailing them!

Venues

Party venues can be expensive, but they also simplify your life a lot by providing everything you need—from entertainment and decor to food and a place to open presents—in one place, and they eliminate the cleanup that comes from hosting a party at home. Because Mandi and her husband live in a rural area that would require their children's friends to drive thirty to forty-five minutes to attend a party, they usually hold their birthday parties in a more central location, either at a park picnic shelter or at a pizza place. The cost of these venues is less than an actual hosted party but still provides many of the same benefits.

Wrapping Paper

Save money on wrapping paper by making your own rather than buying it. Let your kids color or stamp plain butcher paper, wrap your gifts in newspaper and tie with a pretty bow, or make your own reusable fabric gift bags. We love these shabby-chic newspaper gift bags from HowAboutOrange.com too (http://allingoodtime.net/newspaperbags)

WEDDINGS

Weddings can be ridiculously expensive, but you can save a lot of money if you're willing to do some of the legwork yourself. That doesn't mean it has to be stressful, though. The key to getting through the wedding-planning process is to plan early rather than waiting until the last minute. When Mandi and her husband were engaged, her mom insisted that they have everything done a month before their wedding date so that they could "sit around and eat bonbons" in the days leading up to the wedding, and staying on track to do that really reduced the stress as the date got closer.

Cake

Believe it or not, you can actually order a wedding cake from the grocery-store bakery! Mandi and her husband got both their wedding cake and groom's cake from the local grocery store, and they even had the bakery bake wedding-cake charm pulls right into the bottom layer (each of their bridesmaids pulled a good-luck charm out of the cake before they cut it). Not only were the cakes still beautiful, but they were delicious as well!

Flowers

Flowers add a beautiful touch to any wedding, but they can also increase the budget fairly significantly. Save on flowers by making your own arrangements. One option is silk arrangements that you can make yourself ahead of time. Alternatively, a friend of Mandi's actually purchased dozens and dozens of midnight roses from Costco for her wedding, and a group of her family and friends worked together to make her flower arrangements. Fiftyflowers.com is an online wholesale flower distributor that offers very competitive prices on bulk flower purchases.

Photography

Photography is the one area where we don't recommend skimping. Your wedding pictures are a priceless keepsake, and you don't want to look back and regret that you pinched pennies instead of hiring the photographer you really wanted!

Reception

If a dinner reception isn't in your budget, schedule your wedding so that you can serve cake and appetizers instead of a full meal. If you're getting married in a church, see if they have a hall that you can use for your reception rather than moving to a separate venue. You'll also get better pricing on Fridays and Sundays and earlier in the day, since Saturday nights are the most popular time for weddings. To save even more, plan to get married in the off-season between November and April since most weddings are held in the early summer or fall months.

Clutter-Free Gifts

If your family is anything like ours, your kids probably have too many toys, and your house probably has too much stuff. Holidays and birthdays can be stressful because they mean more stuff, but there are plenty of great clutter-free gifts that you can add to your wish list or give to others:

- shared experiences
- crafts supplies
- practical gifts (hair bows, gloves-and-scarf set, etc.)

- lessons or activities
- family memberships
- big-ticket items for the whole family
- contribution to a college fund

Tara and her husband initially planned to get married in St. Lucia, but after some travel issues popped up, they scrapped that idea. Instead, knowing that their family would already be in town for the holiday weekend, they opted to get married on the Friday evening following Thanksgiving. Tara purchased her dress from an online retailer for $299, a gorgeous knockoff of the dress Jennifer Aniston wore when she married Brad Pitt. Tara's bouquet was orange roses from a discount florist in town. And they got married in a simple ceremony at a small chapel downtown, followed by a reception at a local Italian eatery. Her mom made their wedding cake, which she decorated with orange roses to match Tara's bouquet. To top it off, they purchased a Lenox wedding Christmas ornament to use as a cake topper, which then doubled as a cherished ornament for their tree.

Creative Thank-You Cards

Writing thank-you cards may be a dying art, but they're still a thoughtful way to express your appreciation for gifts you receive. Here are a few creative ways to send thank-you cards:

Although we don't recommend sending your boss a fill-in-the-blank thank-you card, printing or ordering a pack of cards that are ready for your child to fill in is perfectly acceptable, especially for younger children who aren't yet great writers.

When Mandi was in college, she nannied for newborn triplets, and their mom would take pictures of them with every gift to send with her thank-you cards. We love that personal touch, and you could simplify it even further by printing the photos out on card stock or postcard paper and mailing them directly to the gift giver with just a little note on the back!

APPENDIX

HOMEMADE CLEANING SUPPLIES

Clorox Anywhere

1 ½ teaspoons of bleach

22 oz. water

Fill spray bottle with water and then add bleach. Put the nozzle on the bottle and shake gently to mix.

Produce Wash

3 parts water

1 part vinegar

Mix in a spray bottle and store under your sink with a produce brush. We recommend using organic vinegar for this since some vinegar is petroleum based, and manufacturers aren't required to disclose this on their labels.

Oven Cleaner

2 cups baking soda

1 cup washing soda

1 teaspoon dish soap

1 tablespoon white vinegar

Mix all ingredients until they form a paste. Then apply thickly to the sides and bottom of your oven and let sit overnight. In the morning, use a wet cloth to scrub the sides until they're clean. Although this is a nontoxic cleaner, you'll still want to wear gloves while you use it!

Homemade Foaming Hand Soap

Foaming hand-soap dispenser

Castile soap

Water, straight from the tap

Add one to two tablespoons of castile soap to the dispenser and then fill it with water. That's it!

Homemade Laundry Detergent

1 bar of Zote (14 oz.)

1 bar of Fels-Naptha (5 oz.)

4 cups Borax

4 cups washing soda (NOT baking soda)

To start, slice each of the bars into three to four pieces and either hand grate them or run them through a food processor until finely ground. Then, combine all four ingredients in a large, sturdy container with a lid, and you're ready to go!

Homemade Dish Detergent

1 part Borax
1 part baking soda

Mix equal parts Borax and baking soda. Add two tablespoons of the mixture to each load of dishes. If you're worried about streaking or spotting, use vinegar as a rinse aid in your dishwasher.

Be sure to rinse your dishes thoroughly before putting them in the dishwasher; this cleaner may not be as effective at getting hard food off of your dishes since it doesn't contain the chemicals of traditional detergents.

Stainless-Steel Cleaner

baby oil
a soft cloth

Put a small amount of baby oil on a dry rag.

Rub it over the surface of the stainless steel in long, even strokes.

Buff off the excess baby oil with a second dry cloth. Be sure to get all of the excess baby oil off or it will attract lint.

Wipe with a dry cloth whenever you notice smudges or streaks.

Repeat every week or two as needed.

Occasionally, clean the whole thing with Windex or vinegar to remove any excess oil and then start fresh.

All-Purpose Cleaner

1 part water

1 part vinegar

drop of essential oil

Dilute white vinegar with equal parts water in an empty spray bottle and use it in place of all-purpose cleaners, disinfectants, and glass cleaners. Add a couple drops of essential oil to cover the smell.

COMMON KITCHEN SUBSTITUTES

Ingredient	Amount	Substitution
allspice	1 teaspoon	½ teaspoon cinnamon, ¼ teaspoon ginger, and ¼ teaspoon cloves
baking powder	1 teaspoon	¼ teaspoon baking soda plus ½ teaspoon cream of tartar
bread crumbs	1 cup	1 cup cracker crumbs or ground oats
buttermilk	1 cup	1 tablespoon lemon juice or vinegar plus enough milk to make 1 cup
corn syrup	1 cup	1 ¼ cup sugar plus ⅓ cup water OR 1 cup honey
heavy cream	1 cup	¾ cup milk plus ⅓ cup butter OR 1 cup evaporated milk
cream cheese	1 cup	1 cup pureed cottage cheese
cream of tartar	1 teaspoon	2 teaspoons lemon juice or vinegar
egg	1 whole	½ banana mashed with ½ teaspoon baking powder OR 2 tablespoons ground flaxseed soaked in 3 tablespoons water OR 2 tablespoons cornstarch
garlic	1 clove	⅛ teaspoon garlic powder
herbs	1 tablespoon fresh	1 teaspoon dried

Ingredient	Amount	Substitution
hot pepper sauce	1 teaspoon	$3/4$ teaspoon cayenne pepper mixed with 1 teaspoon vinegar
ketchup	1 cup	1 cup tomato sauce, 1 teaspoon vinegar, and 1 tablespoon sugar
lemon juice	1 teaspoon	$1/2$ teaspoon vinegar
mayonnaise	1 cup	1 cup plain yogurt
mustard	1 tablespoon	1 tablespoon dried mustard, 1 teaspoon water, 1 teaspoon vinegar, and 1 teaspoon sugar
oil in baked goods	1 cup	1 cup apple sauce or other fruit puree
onion	1 cup, chopped	$1/4$ cup onion powder
shortening	1 cup	1 cup butter
sour cream	1 cup	1 cup plain yogurt OR 1 tablespoon lemon juice or vinegar plus enough cream to make 1 cup
soy sauce	1/2 cup	4 tablespoons Worcestershire sauce plus 1 tablespoon water
vinegar	1 teaspoon	1 teaspoon lemon juice
wine	1 cup	1 cup broth OR 1 cup fruit juice plus 2 teaspoons vinegar
yogurt	1 cup	1 cup sour cream OR 1 cup buttermilk

PANTRY INVENTORY

BASICS

coffee and tea

dried beans

flour

grains

jam or jelly

nut butter

nuts

oil

pasta

specialty sauces

sugar

vinegar

yeast

SPICES

allspice

basil

bay leaves

cardamom

celery seeds

cinnamon

cumin

dill

oregano

parsley

pepper

rosemary

salt

BAKING

baking powder

baking soda

chocolate chips or chunks

cocoa powder

cornstarch

cream of tartar

vanilla extract

FREEZER STORAGE TIPS

breads & desserts

angel food, sponge cake	2 mos.
bread, rolls	3–6 mos.
cheesecake	2–3 mos.
cookie dough	4 mos.
cookies (baked)	6–8 mos.
pies (baked)	1–2 mos.
quick bread, muffins	2–3 mos.
yellow or pound cake	6 mos.

fish & seafood

clams, mussels, oysters (live)	2–3 mos.
clams, mussels, oysters (shucked)	3–6 mos.
fish (cooked)	4–6 mos.
fish (fatty)	2–3 mos.
fish (lean)	4–6 mos.
shellfish	2–3 mos.
shrimp, scallops	4–6 mos.

poultry

casseroles	4–6 mos.
chicken or turkey (cooked)	4–6 mos.
chicken or turkey (ground)	3–4 mos.
chicken or turkey (pieces)	6–8 mos.

dairy

butter	6–9 mos.
cottage cheese	1 mos.
cheese (hard)	6 mos.
cheese (soft)	4–6 mos.
eggs	6–8 mos.
ice cream, sherbet	2 mos.
milk, cream	3–4 mos.
yogurt	1–2 mos.

meats

bacon, sausage (raw)	1–2 mos.
ham (cooked)	1–2 mos.
lunch meat	1–2 mos.
casseroles, soups	2–3 mos.
ground beef, pork	3–4 mos.
chops, roasts	4–6 mos.
steaks	8–10 mos.

produce

fruit (citrus)	3–4 mos.
fruit (other)	12 mos.
fruit juice (concentrate)	12 mos.
fruit juice (bottled)	8–12 mos.

FREEZER TIPS

Keep your freezer temperature at 0 degrees or less.

Seal food in airtight containers or packages.

Label containers with use by date and cooking instructions.

Group similar items on your freezer shelves.

Rotate your freezer stock each time you grocery shop, moving the oldest items forward.

Food should not be thawed and refrozen, but can be thawed, cooked, and then refrozen.

INTERNAL COOKING TEMPERATURES

beef and lamb (160 ° F)

roasts, steaks, & chops:

rare	120–125° F	center is bright red, pinkish outside
medium rare	130–135° F	center is very pink, slightly brown outside
medium	140–145° F	center is light pink, brown outside
medium well	150–155° F	not pink
well done	160° F +	steak is uniformly brown throughout
ground meat	160–165° F	uniformly brown throughout

poultry (165 ° F)

chicken & duck	165° F	cook until juices run clear
turkey	165° F	juices run clear—leg moves easily
stuffing	165° F	

pork (160 ° F)

roasts, steaks, & chops:

medium	140–145° F	pale pink center
well done	160° F +	steak is uniformly brown throughout
ribs, shoulders & brisket	160° F +	medium to well done

pork (160 ° F)

sausage (raw)	160° F	no longer pink
ham:		
raw	160° F	
precooked	140° F	

fish and seafood (145 ° F)

fish	140° F	flesh is opaque, flakes easily
tuna, swordfish, & marlin	125° F	cook until medium rare
shrimp:		
medium-size, boiling	3–4 min.	cook until medium rare
Large size, boiling	5–7 min.	cook until medium rare
Jumbo size, boiling	7–8 min.	cook until medium rare
lobster:		
boiled, whole (1 lb.)	12–15 min.	meat turns red, opaque center when cut
broiled, whole (1½ lbs.)	3–4 min.	meat turns red, opaque center when cut
steamed, whole (1½ lbs.)	15–20 min.	meat turns red, opaque center when cut
baked, tails (each)	15 min.	meat turns red, opaque center when cut
broiled, tails (each)	9–10 min.	meat turns red, opaque center when cut
scallops:		
baked	12–15 min.	milky white or opaque, and firm
broiled		milky white or opaque, and firm
clams, mussels, & oysters		when their shells open

SEASONAL PRODUCE

SPRING

apricots	fennel	rhubarb
artichokes	fiddlehead	shallots
asparagus	green beans	snow peas
avocados	head or iceberg	sorrel
basil	lettuce	spinach
beans	honeydew	spring baby lettuce
beets	limes	squash
berries	mango	strawberries
broccoli	morel mushrooms	sugar snap peas
cabbage	mustard greens	summer squash
chili peppers	okra	sweet corn
Chinese cabbage	oranges	sweet oranges
chives	papayas	sweet peppers
collard greens	peas	Swiss chard
cucumbers	pineapple	turnips
English peas	radish	Vidalia onions
fava beans	ramps	watercress

SUMMER

apricots	blackberries	chili peppers
basil	blueberries	corn
beans	boysenberries	crenshaw melon
beets	cantaloupe	cucumbers
bell peppers	casaba melon	dates
berries	cherries	eggplant

figs	loganberries	strawberries
garlic	mangoes	summer squash
grapefruit	melons	sweet corn
grapes	nectarines	sweet peppers
green beans	okra	tomatillo
green peas	peaches	tomatoes
honeydew melons	Persian melons	watermelon
kiwifruit	plums	zucchini
lima beans	radishes	
limes	raspberries	

FALL

acorn squash	dates	parsnips
apples	daikon radish	pears
Belgian endive	fennel	persimmons
bok choy	garlic	pineapple
broccoli	ginger	pomegranates
brussels sprouts	grapes	pumpkin
butternut squash	greens	quince
cabbage	guava	rutabagas
cauliflower	head or iceberg	shallots
celery root	lettuce	spinach
chayote squash	huckleberries	star fruit
cherimoya	kohlrabi	sweet peppers
chicory	kumquats	sweet potatoes
chili peppers	leaf lettuce	Swiss chard
Chinese cabbage	mandarin oranges	turnips
coconuts	mushrooms	winter squash
cranberries	nuts	yams
cucumbers	okra	

WINTER

apples	Chinese cabbage	persimmons
Belgian endive	coconuts	pummelo
bok choy	dates	radicchio
broccoli	fennel	red currants
brussels sprouts	grapefruit	rutabagas
cabbage	kale	spinach
cauliflower	leeks	sweet potatoes
celery root	mushrooms	tangerines
cherimoya	oranges	turnips
chestnuts	parsnips	winter squash
chicory	pear	yams

YEAR-ROUND

avocados	celery	papayas
bananas	lemons	bell peppers
cabbage	lettuce	potatoes
carrots	onions	

NECESSITIES FOR YOUR . . .

UTENSIL DRAWER

measuring cups

measuring spoons

liquid measuring cup

paring knife

chef's knife

serrated knife

vegetable peeler

kitchen shears

ladle

whisk

slotted spoon

wooden spoon

rubber/metal spatula

tongs

can opener

MEDICINE CABINET

ibuprofen

decongestant

antihistamine

topical antibiotic cream

Band-Aids

thermometer

tweezers

saline nose spray

children's ibuprofen

ice pack

TOOL KIT

hammer

tape measure

Phillips-head screwdriver

flathead screwdriver

Allen wrenches

pliers

adjustable wrench

level

OFFICE

pens

pencils

highlighters

paper clips

Post-it notes

thumb tacks

ruler

scissors

calculator

postage stamps

hole punch

CLEANING KIT

microfiber cloths

all-purpose spray (or vinegar)

glass spray (or vinegar)

old toothbrush

toilet brush

DEEP-CLEANING CHECKLISTS

KITCHEN

Declutter

COOKBOOKS

Make copies of any recipes you don't want to lose.

Create a notebook or digitize them with a program like Plan to Eat.

Donate cookbooks that you don't use regularly.

PANTRY

Clean out expired food and trash it.

Donate canned and boxed goods you're not going to use.

Organize the items in your pantry with the earliest expiration dates in the front.

Group items by category—baking, dinner, snacks, spices, etc.

Make a list of pantry staples to stock up for the holidays.

FRIDGE

Toss expired condiments and old food.

DRAWERS/CABINETS

Declutter appliances, pots/pans, and kitchen tools. (How often do you really use it? Is there something else you could use instead?)

Get rid of duplicates unless you really use them.

Declutter storage containers/lids and get rid of the ones that are missing their other half.

Create "zones" for your tools so they're close to where you actually use them—a coffee zone, a baking zone, a cooking zone, etc.

Cleaning

Start at the top—dust the tops of cabinets, appliances, and range hoods.

Vacuum/wipe down cabinet shelves, drawers, and your pantry.

Use vinegar/water to clean the shelves in your fridge/freezer.

Clean your oven.

Clean under your oven (often the drawer will pull right out so you can get under there).

Clean behind your fridge if possible. Take off the front grill and clean it out to make it more efficient.

Clean your stove/range. Soak inserts in vinegar to loosen the grime or use stove-top cleaner for flat-top stoves.

Clean stainless-steel appliances with baby oil.

Clean any glass or windows in your kitchen (cabinet doors or shelves, oven doors, picture frames, etc.).

Dust knickknacks and baseboards.

Maintaining

Keep a pantry inventory to keep track of items you need to replenish.

Try menu planning so you're not buying extras you won't use.

Clean out your fridge each week before you go grocery shopping and wipe down the shelves as you do.

Line the bottom of your oven with foil to catch drips and spills.

Clean up stove spills/boil-overs right away so they don't build up or harden.

Get into a habit of running your dishwasher regularly and emptying it right away so that your dirty dishes don't pile up in the sink.

Clean up every night so you don't start the next day with a mess in the kitchen, à la FlyLady.

Rotate your stockpile regularly.

Use glass storage containers. They're healthier AND you can see what's in them.

FAMILY & LIVING ROOM

Declutter

MEDIA

Clean out video games, movies that you no longer watch or the kids have grown out of.

Consider giving up the original cases in favor of CD books to save space.

Get rid of extras—remotes, consoles, cords, etc.

Consider a basket or caddy for corralling remotes.

Label cords with a label maker. Wrap up excess wire with a twisty tie. Plug plugs in relative to their location and make the things you're likely to unplug easily accessible.

TOYS

Designate an area for toys if you want to keep some in your family room. Use a basket, toy box, or cabinet to store them so they're not just spread around the room.

Return extra toys to bedrooms/playrooms regularly.

Create sets you can rotate rather than trying to keep them all out at once.

BOOKSHELVES & KNICKKNACKS

Clean off shelves and get rid of accumulated stuff that's been set down on flat surfaces over time.

Donate books that you've read but don't want to keep.

Read and donate extra magazines. If you have a ton to catch up on, limit yourself to three months of back issues.

Consider paring back the number of knickknacks you have. The less you keep out on shelves and tables, the less you have to dust.

Cleaning

Dust ceiling fans and reverse their direction to push the hot air down.

Dust high shelves, window and door frames.

Dust your entertainment center, TV, and electronics.

Dust shelves and knickknacks.

Clean the windows, mirrors, TV screen.

Spot-clean your upholstery and carpet.

Clean under couch cushions and under the couch.

Wipe baseboards.

Vacuum and/or mop.

Maintaining

Clean up toys every day (once or twice a day) so that the clutter doesn't accumulate over time.

Don't let flat surfaces accumulate stuff. Find a home for everything.

Dust and clean glass/mirrors weekly.

BATHROOM

Declutter

BATH TOYS

Throw away squirty toys because they can harbor mildew and mold.

Stick other bath toys in the dishwasher on a sanitize cycle to get them really clean.

Consider cutting back the number of bath toys you keep in the bathroom and rotating them from time to time.

STOCKPILE

Organize your stockpile in your linen closet so you can actually see what you have.

Put the earliest expiration date in the front to be sure you use it before it expires.

Donate products you won't use or have an abundance of.

Consider moving your stockpile OUT of the bathroom or linen closet and into the garage or basement if you have space.

MEDICINES

Throw away expired medicines (be sure to follow the FDA's recommendations for properly disposing of medicine).

Make a list of medicines/homeopathic remedies you need before cold and flu season hits.

Check for droppers, measuring cups, etc., but throw away extras (do you really need seven of each?).

SAMPLES

Only keep the samples you'll actually use. I love to take the packets of shampoo and conditioner when we travel, but there are some samples that I'll probably never use.

Use bags or baskets to organize them by type to make it more likely that you'll use them.

Discard old samples.

TIP: Create a guest basket with samples in case your guests forget something.

Cleaning

Dust high fixtures, windows, shelves, and the top of your bath/shower unit (if it has a ledge).

Wipe the shelves in closets/cabinets/drawers while you're decluttering.

Add cleaner to the toilet bowl and let it soak while you clean the rest of the bathroom.

Clean mirrors.

Clean the sink, especially around fixtures.

Clean shower walls and doors to remove soap scum.

Scrub the tub/shower floor.

Dust baseboards.

Clean the outside of the toilet and the toilet seat.

Scrub the inside of the toilet bowl.

Mop.

Maintaining

Limit the number of bath toys in the tub at a time.

Wipe down the sink every day. We use my husband's towel from his shower (he's supposed to be clean when he gets out, right?) or you could keep rags under the sink to use.

Don't sign up for free samples just because you can unless you really think you'll use them.

Keep a written inventory of medicine so you don't find out you're out of ibuprofen at one o'clock in the morning with a feverish kid.

Clean the bathroom while bathing your kids.

BEDROOMS

Declutter

CLOTHES

Most people wear 20 percent of their wardrobe 80 percent of the time. If you don't like something in your closet, you probably won't ever like it, so pass it on.

Turn all of your hangers around backward and then, when you wear something, hang it up the right way. You'll be able to quickly see what you never wear.

Make a list of any essentials you need for the holiday season so you can watch for sales on those items rather than having to rush out at the last minute to purchase them.

Pack away your seasonal wardrobe so that you have more space in your dresser and closet.

FLAT SURFACES

Scale back the number of knickknacks and mementos you keep in your bedroom so that only your favorites are left.

Clean off flat surfaces and find homes for the things you tend to just set down.

Sort through books and magazines and give away any that you won't read again.

STORAGE

If you use your master bedroom as a catchall for anything that doesn't have a home, sort through the piles and find homes for the items. Your bedroom should be a haven so that you can truly rest and recharge.

Empty the closet shelves and sort through any long-term storage.

In the guest room, organize and sort through your storage to create an inviting—rather than cluttered—space for your guests.

Cleaning

Wash mattress covers and replace any old or worn-out pillows.

Wash sheets and hang comforters outside to air out.

Dust ceiling fans and reverse fan direction.

Dust high shelves, window and door frames.

Dust dressers/TVs.

Dust shelves/knickknacks.

Clean blinds and shades.

Clean windows/mirrors/screens.

Spot-clean upholstery and carpet.

Clean under/behind the couch.

Wipe baseboards.

Vacuum and/or mop.

Maintaining

Don't let flat surfaces accumulate stuff; find a home for it.

Don't use your master bedroom as a catchall.

Dust and clean glass/mirrors weekly.

Pass on any clothes that you haven't worn after six to eight weeks unless they're special-occasion items.

KIDS' ROOMS

Declutter

CLOTHES

Sort through kids clothes and organize them by size.

Set aside any pieces that don't have a match—skirts that don't have a matching shirt, etc.—and either purchase a match or give them away.

Turn all of the hangers around backward and hang things the proper way after they're worn so you can see what's being worn and what's not.

Make a list of any essentials the kids need for the holiday.

Pack away seasonal wardrobes to make more space in dressers and closets.

TOYS

Involve kids in the process rather than doing it behind their backs.

Purge the toys to make room for new toys.

Throw away broken pieces.

Group sets together.

Give away toys that don't get played with.

Set limits on miscellaneous toys. For example, we have a bag that all of the little toys we pick up from Happy Meals—an occasional treat, birthday parties, etc. go into. When the bag gets full, we go through and choose which to give away and which to keep.

If you have a collector in the family, give them a defined space for their collection and then help them make the tough decisions if their collection is too large for the space.

DESKS & HOMEWORK AREAS
Repair or recycle torn books.

Throw away any empty glue bottles, unusable pencils, etc.

Dust or vacuum inside drawers.

File or recycle papers.

Sort supplies and pack away extras to reduce clutter.

Cleaning

Wash mattress covers and replace any old or worn-out pillows.

Wash sheets and hang comforters outside to air out.

Dust ceiling fans and reverse fan direction.

Dust high shelves, window and door frames.

Dust dressers/TVs.

Dust shelves/knickknacks.

Clean blinds and shades.

Clean windows/mirrors/screens.

Spot-clean carpet.

Wipe baseboards.

Vacuum and/or mop.

Maintaining

Consider a family closet for kids' clothing if they're not old enough to take responsibility for putting things away themselves yet.

Follow the one-toy-in, one-toy-out rule and give away a toy each time a new one is received.

Clean up every day and put toys away by set so that the mess doesn't build up over time.

Rotate toys every one to two months rather than having them all available all the time.

Request clutter-free gifts like craft supplies, experiences, and books (you'll never convince me that children's books are clutter!).

Give kids regular age-appropriate chores and have them help maintain their areas.

STORAGE AREAS

Declutter

SENTIMENTAL

If you're keeping things because you can't bear to part with them, unpack them and find a use for them in your home rather than keeping them hidden away.

It's okay to save mementos that pass on your family history to the next generation, but don't hold on to things just because you're afraid you'll lose the memories if you part with the item.

If you haven't thought about an item in a long time and don't have any use for it now, give it away.

Keep a box for each of your children of special things from their childhood, but limit yourself to one box.

EXTRAS

Think about how long something has been in storage and how likely you are to need it in the near future in order to make an objective decision about keeping it.

Ask yourself how much it would cost to replace it if you happen to need it at some point.

Ask yourself how easy it would be to find a replacement if needed.

HAND-ME-DOWNS

Organize hand-me-downs by size/gender so that they're not just sitting in storage gathering dust because you've forgotten about them.

Go through hand-me-downs and give away any that you don't truly love. Chances are if you don't love it in the box, you're not gonna love it when it comes time for your child to wear it either.

Remember that there are people who could use your hand-me-downs. Consider lending or giving away any that you're not currently using.

SEASONAL DECOR

Give away any seasonal decor that stays in the box year after year.

Cleaning

Clean behind boxes and bins. Vacuum, dust corners, and wipe down walls if necessary.

Wipe down shelves.

Group boxes by season or size so that it's easy to find them.

Label boxes clearly with detailed descriptions of what's inside.

Pack seasonal decor by room or type so that all of your ornaments are together, all of your living room decor is together, etc.

Maintaining

Think twice before putting something in storage—do you really need to keep it? Is it worth the cost of storing it, the time you'll have to invest to take care of it, and the space you're giving up?

When you take something out of storage, be sure to put it back in the correctly labeled box when you're done.

Store your regular decor in your holiday boxes so they'll be easy to find when it's time to pack the seasonal/holiday decor away.

INTERNET RESOURCES

BACKYARD

AAA.com

Amazon.com

AutoTrader.com

Better Business Bureau (BBB.org)

CarsDirect.com

Craigslist.com

eBay.com

GardenGuides.com

GardenMandy.com

GardensAblaze.com

InsectLore.com

Kelley Blue Book (KBB.com)

Motors.eBay.com

National Climatic Data Center (ncdc.noaa.gov)

TireRack.com

BASEMENT

GreenLivingOnline.com

LaundryTree.com

OneSuite.com

BATHROOM

1800Contacts.com

American Cancer Society (Cancer.org)

AmyLovesIt.com

EyesLipsFace.com

JustEyewear.com

National Association of Boards of Pharmacy (NABP.net)

National Cancer Institute (Cancer.gov)

NationalBreastCancer.org

OhAmanda.com

SamaritanMinistries.org

SpaWeek.com

ZenniOptical.com

BEDROOM

Etsy.com

FortheMommas.com

KangarooKeeper.com

Lifehacker.com

MarthaStewart.com

Pouchee.com

RealSimple.com

SleepFoundation.org

SnapTotes.com

DINING ROOM / LIVING ROOM

ClutterDiet.com

Craigslist.com

FlyLady.net

Habitat.org/Restores

Heloise.com

MarthaStewart.com

Movex.com

MyBlessedLife.net

OrgJunkie.com

SimpleMom.net

SimpleOrganic.net

SimpleOrganizedLiving.com

HOME OFFICE

BecomingMinimalist.com

CellPhonesforSoldiers.com

Coinstar.com

ConsumerReports.org

Couponizer.com

Cozi.com

DaveRamsey.com

DMAChoice.org

Dropbox.com

GetHuman.com

GetRichSlowly.org

INGDirect.com

KidsProtectionPlan.com

MobileMe (Me.com)

National Coalition Against Domestic Violence
(NCADV.org)

OptOutScreening.com

Phones4Life.org

RebateTracker.com

Rent-A-Text.com

ShopSmartMag.org

SquareTrade.com

Swagbucks.com

WAHM.com

WorkPlaceLikeHome.com

KIDS

BabyCheapskate.com

BusyBodyBook.com

HSLDA.org

LifeAsMom.com

NurtureBaby.com

Recalls.gov

SeatCheck.org

SimpleHomeschool.net

SimpleKids.net

WholesomeBabyFood.com

KITCHEN

FoodforMyFamily.com

OnceaMonthMom.com

PlantoEat.com

SimpleBites.net

Unsophisticook.com

REC ROOM

AllEars.net

Amazon.com

American Kennel Club (AKC.org)

FareCompare.com

GasBuddy.com

Google.com/Products

HomesforSwap.com

iTunes.com

Kayak.com

MouseSavers.com

National Park Service (NPS.gov)

Netflix.com

NexTag.com

Pandora.com

PriceGrabber.com

Redbox.com

Restaurants.com

ScoreBig.com

Southwest Airlines (Southwest.com)

TheMouseforLess.com

TourGuideMike.com

WDWInfo.com

HOLIDAYS/EVENTS

100DaystoChristmas.com

HowAboutOrange.com

RECOMMENDED READING

Clutter Rehab by Laura Wittman (http://allingoodtime.net/clutterrehab)

Mommy Made and Daddy Too! by Martha & David Kimmel (http://allingoodtime.net/mommymade)

Organized Simplicity by Tsh Oxenreider (http://allingood time.net/organizedsimplicity)

Steady Days by Jamie Martin (http://allingoodtime.net/steadydays)

Super Baby Food by Ruth Yaron (http://allingoodtime.net/superbabyfood)

The Total Money Makeover by Dave Ramsey (http://allin goodtime.net/totalmoneymakeover)

The Unofficial Guide Walt Disney World 2011 by Bob Seh-linger (http://allingoodtime.net/unofficialguide)

Wear Clean Underwear!: A Fast, Fun, Friendly and Essential Guide to Legal Planning for Busy Parents by Alexis Martin Neely (http://allingoodtime.net/estateplanning)

Your Money: The Missing Manual by J. D. Roth (http://allin goodtime.net/yourmoney)

QUICK LINKS

BACKYARD

Backyard Botanical Oasis Garden (http://allingoodtime.net/oasis)

Companion Planting (http://allingoodtime.net/companionplanting)

Garage Sale Classifieds (http://allingoodtime.net/garagesales)

Motion-activated Scarecrow Sprinkler (http://allingoodtime.net/scarecrow)

National Climatic Data Center (http://allingoodtime.net/NCDC)

Organic DIY Pesticides (http://allingoodtime.net/pesticides)

The Entertainment Book (http://allingoodtime.net/entertainmentbook)

BATHROOM

Folding Linens (http://allingoodtime.net/linens)

Free Antibiotics & Discounted Prescriptions (http://allingoodtime.net/prescriptions)

Spa Week (http://allingoodtime.net/spaweek)

Sunscreen versus Sun Block (http://allingoodtime.net/sunscreen)

VIPPS-accredited Pharmacies (http://allingoodtime.net/VIPPS)

Weekly Drugstore Deals (http://allingoodtime.net/drugstores)

ZeroWater Treatment System (http://allingoodtime.net/zerowater)

BEDROOM

Reputable Purse Dealers (http://allingoodtime.net/purses)

Benefits of Lemon Water (http://allingoodtime.net/lemonwater)

DINING ROOM / LIVING ROOM

Dyson Vacuums (http://allingoodtime.net/dyson)

KIDS

Amazon Mom (http://allingoodtime.net/amazonmom)

BusyBodyBook Planner (http://allingoodtime.net/busybodybook)

Cloth Diapers (http://allingoodtime.net/clothdiapers)

Diaper Deals (http://allingoodtime.net/diapers)

DIY LEGO Table (http://allingoodtime.net/legotable)

Donna Young's Homeschool Planner (http://allingoodtime.net/donnayoung)

Homeschool Tracker (http://allingoodtime.net/homeschooltracker)

Melissa & Doug Chore Chart (http://allingoodtime.net/cho rechart)

Money Management Piggy Bank (http://allingoodtime.net/ piggybank)

Printable Chore Chart (http://allingoodtime.net/printable chorechart)

HOME OFFICE

Couponizer (http://allingoodtime.net/couponizer)

Dropbox (http://allingoodtime.net/dropbox)

iCloud (http://allingoodtime.net/icloud)

iGo Power Savers (http://allingoodtime.net/igo)

ING Direct (http://allingoodtime.net/ingdirect)

Paper File System (http://allingoodtime.net/filing)

Photo Printing Deals (http://allingoodtime.net/photoprints)

Printable Home Inventory (http://allingoodtime.net/home inventory)

KITCHEN

BluApple (http://allingoodtime.net/bluapple)

Deal Seeking Mom Coupon Database (http://allingoodtime .net/coupondatabase)

Plan to Eat (http://allingoodtime.net/plantoeat)

Produce Storage Tips (http://allingoodtime.net/produce)

REC ROOM

Amazon Video on Demand (http://allingoodtime.net/video ondemand)

Birthday Deals (http://allingoodtime.net/birthdaydeals)

Cash-Back Sites (http://allingoodtime.net/cashback)

Daily Deals Sites (http://allingoodtime.net/dailydeals)

Kids Eat Free (http://allingoodtime.net/kidseatfree)

Netflix (http://allingoodtime.net/netflix)

Printable Packing Lists (http://allingoodtime.net/packing list)

Redbox Codes (http://allingoodtime.net/redbox)

Swag Bucks (http://allingoodtime.net/swagbucks)

Tax Software (http://allingoodtime.net/taxsoftware)

Wrapping Electronic Cords (http://allingoodtime.net/cords)

HOLIDAYS & EVENT PLANNING

Cake Pops (http://allingoodtime.net/cakepops)

Holiday Planners (http://allingoodtime.net/holidayebooks)

Newspaper Gift Bags (http://allingoodtime.net/newspaper bags)

If you enjoyed the tips, tricks, and advice contained in this book, we invite you to subscribe to our blogs to continue your journey in saving time and money. We invite you to visit us at allingoodtime.net and to subscribe to our blogs to continue your journey in saving time and money:

Deal Seeking Mom
http://dealseekingmom.com

Unsophisticook
http://unsophisticook.com

Life . . . Your Way
http://lifeyourway.net

Jungle Deals & Steals
http://jungledealsandsteals.com

If you have questions or suggestions, we'd love to hear from you:

contact@allingoodtime.net